# EPIC ATHLETES
# SIMONE BILES

# Dan Wetzel
## Illustrations by Marcelo Baez

Henry Holt and Company
New York

*For Cameron Williams*

Henry Holt and Company, Publishers since 1866
Henry Holt® is a registered trademark of Macmillan Publishing Group, LLC
120 Broadway, New York, NY 10271 • mackids.com

Library of Congress Cataloging-in-Publication Data
Names: Wetzel, Dan, author. | Baez, Marcelo, illustrator. | Wetzel, Dan. Epic athletes. |
Henry Holt and Company.
Title: Epic athletes : Simone Biles / Dan Wetzel ; illustrations by Marcelo Baez.
Other titles: Simone Biles
Description: First Edition. | New York : Henry Holt Books for Young Readers, 2020. |
Series: Epic athletes ; 7 | Audience: Ages: 8-12 years Audience: Grades: 2-3 | Summary:
"The seventh book in a middle-grade nonfiction sports series that focuses on today's
superstars and up-and-comers" —Provided by publisher.
Identifiers: LCCN 2019041367 | ISBN 9781250295828 (Hardcover)
Subjects: LCSH: Biles, Simone, 1997– —Juvenile literature. | Women gymnasts—United
States—Biography—Juvenile literature. | Gymnasts—United States—Biography—Juvenile
literature. | African American women athletes—United States—Biography—Juvenile
literature. | Women Olympic athletes—United States—Biography—Juvenile literature. |
Olympic Games (31st : 2016 : Rio de Janeiro, Brazil)—Juvenile literature.
Classification: LCC GV460.2.B55 W48 2020 | DDC 796.44092 [B]—dc23
LC record available at https://lccn.loc.gov/2019041367

Our books may be purchased in bulk for promotional, educational, or business use.
Please contact your local bookseller or the Macmillan Corporate and
Premium Sales Department at (800) 221-7945 ext. 5442 or by email
at MacmillanSpecialMarkets@macmillan.com.

First edition, 2020 / Designed by Elynn Cohen
Printed in the United States of America
by LSC Communications, Harrisonburg, Virginia
1  3  5  7  9  10  8  6  4  2

THE 2016 OLYMPICS WOMEN'S GYMNASTICS
ALL-AROUND FINAL

# 1

# Golden

SIMONE BILES, IN HER custom-fit, red, white, and blue leotard, stood on one end of the mat, her left hand high in the air, her right resting on her hip.

Twelve thousand fans stared down at her inside Rio Olympic Arena in Brazil, everyone hushed and quiet as they waited for the music to start and Simone to begin a ninety-second floor routine that might tumble her right into history.

The then-nineteen-year-old from the suburbs of Houston, Texas, was in the lead at the women's all-around gymnastics competition at the 2016

Olympics. All that remained was her strongest event—floor. Do it well and she'd be crowned champion.

There were Olympic rings hanging on a banner overhead. There was a gold medal waiting to be hung around someone's neck. There was anticipation in the air as spectators wondered what type of show the greatest gymnast of all time would stage. She was a tiny figure in the middle of a huge arena, an American dynamo who stood just four foot eight.

"I tell people four foot nine sometimes," she once said with a laugh.

To say this was Simone Biles's lifelong dream, the one that powered her through the days at practice when she lacked motivation, wasn't even true. She had never actually dreamed this far. Olympic champion? Gold medalist? The greatest of all time? That was too much to conceive, even on those quiet nights growing up when she tried to fantasize her way to sleep.

No, as a young gymnast, leaping and cartwheeling through recreation classes and local Junior Olympic meets and even as she climbed the competitive national and international ranks, pushing herself more and more, she aspired only to reach the Olympics.

Just getting here was enough. Winning gold? It somehow never crossed her mind.

Simone was a planner. She liked to write down goals in a small notebook she kept in her bedroom back in Spring, Texas. It could be about achieving a certain grade in a certain class, something related to gymnastics, or another milestone. It was a way to keep her focused. It was a way to keep her going.

Yet once she qualified for her first Olympics a few weeks prior to the 2016 games in Rio de Janeiro, there was nothing else she had written down that remained to be accomplished. She had already been national champion four times and world champion three. She had already turned professional. She had already signed contracts that would make her millions in endorsement deals.

Her mother, Nellie, was concerned that Simone might not perform well if she didn't jot down the ultimate goal—Olympic champion in the all-around. That gold signifies the best in the world because it requires each gymnast to perform in all four events—vault, balance beam, uneven bars, and this one, floor exercise. So Nellie encouraged her daughter to put it on paper, make it official.

Simone was hesitant. It seemed unnecessary and

even made her nervous and anxious. She had come to embrace the philosophy of Martha Karolyi, the US national team coordinator and a legendary coach in the sport.

"Martha would say, 'You want to perform like you train. Did you perform like you trained? If you perform like you train, then the judging will work itself out,'" Simone said.

It's a simple lesson that can deliver incredible accomplishments. Do what you can do and don't stress about anything else.

"If I do my job, I do my job," Simone said. "There is nothing I can do to control the scores."

So Simone would only meet her mother halfway. She did write down a new goal, but it had nothing to do with medals or scores or sticking the landing on an Amanar.

"I will make you proud," Simone wrote to her mother.

That was it. That was all. Nellie could only smile when she read it. Simone could have fallen fifty times on her floor routine and she would still be proud of her daughter.

Ron and Nellie Biles were not Simone's birth parents. They were, originally, her grandparents.

Ron Biles had a daughter from a previous relationship named Shanon, who had given birth to four children, including Simone, the third child. Shanon and the kids lived in Ohio, but when Shanon struggled with alcohol and drug addiction, eventually child services said she was an unfit mother and took her children from her, putting them temporarily in foster care.

Ron and Nellie had married after his first relationship broke off, and they were living in Texas at the time. When Shanon was unable to care for her kids, the pair stepped in and adopted the two youngest, Simone and her little sister, Adria. The two older children went with another relative. It wasn't planned this way, but Grandma and Grandpa officially and legally became Simone's mom and dad. Ron and Nellie already had two older boys and now the family was unexpectedly bigger, and given Simone's natural interest in flips and twists, bouncier.

Neither Ron nor Nellie knew anything about gymnastics when Simone and Adria first began going to a local gym to burn off excess energy. They certainly never expected to be here, at the Olympics, staring down at their daughter who was on the verge of winning the all-around gold. It wasn't the athletic success that made them love her, though. It was everything else.

"We have so much satisfaction from all our kids," Ron Biles said. "We love family and everything involved with it. We share all the special moments together and this is a pretty special one."

Down on that mat, Simone was trying to remain calm. She had trained since she was six years old to get to this spot. She had always been a pint-size powerhouse, always small for her age. Yet in elementary school, she was often stronger than the boys and had no problem showing them.

She was pure muscle, with ripped arms and springy legs that launched her into the air. She had a core so strong she could twist in midair almost at will. She also possessed an unteachable ability to sense where she was while in flight.

The routine she was about to attempt was one of the most technically challenging runs of skills in the history of the sport. The Olympics were home to the best gymnasts on earth, yet no other gymnast present would even attempt such a difficult feat.

Simone wasn't just going to try it. She was going to try to do it perfectly.

It began with a full-twisting double layout, where

a gymnast flips in the air with her legs completely straightened out (rather than bending her knees). Next up, a double laid-out salto (a flip with the legs tucked to the chest) with a half twist, a move so hard that no one had ever landed it in a World Championship until Simone had done so in 2013. As a result, it was known as "the Biles."

The Biles led Simone into a split jump and later there was a tumbling pass with a double-double (two somersaults with two full twists) and then the finale with a tucked full-in (two somersaults and a twist with legs pressed together and to the chest). In between the four tumbling runs, there were other required moves, choreographed dancing with a salsa flair, and a beaming smile to engage the crowd.

The routine was so demanding that it earned a 6.800 degree of difficulty, which is one part of a gymnastics score. The other is how the judges think you executed it. No one else in the meet had a difficulty score higher than 6.600.

Simone hadn't lost an individual all-around competition since 2013, yet this one, the Olympic all-around, hadn't been easy. She had led after the first event, vault, but then fell behind Russia's Aliya Mustafina after the second rotation, bars, when

Aliya put up an impressive 15.666, a full 0.7 higher than Simone.

The crowd in Rio de Janeiro mumbled in surprise when Aliya took the overall lead, 30.866 to 30.832. Everyone had expected Simone to run away with the gold, just like always. Now they were wondering if a historic upset was in the making.

Simone's personal coach, Aimee Boorman, told her to just stick with her training. Teammate Aly Raisman, who was also competing in the all-around, high-fived her and tried to pump her up.

And Bela and Martha Karolyi, the legendary husband-and-wife coaching duo who essentially ran USA Gymnastics, reminded Simone that since bars were her weakest event and Aliya's strongest, there was no need to panic. There was plenty of time during the final two events—beam and floor—to retake the lead.

"That made this competition so spicy, so beautiful," said Bela Karolyi, who for over forty years had coached many of the greatest gymnasts of all time. "The beam is the leaning point [though]. The left or the right. The best-trained gymnast stays on the beam."

Well, beam was next. And before Simone's routine,

she heard Nellie Biles shout a saying that she'd been screaming to Simone her entire competitive career.

"You've got this, Simone!" Nellie said.

That was more than enough for Simone. As with the floor event to come, she benefited from having a far more difficult technical routine in the beam than her competitors, tougher than anyone else was even willing to attempt.

She then drilled it, proving herself, as Bela said, "the best-trained gymnast," and scoring a 15.433 to Aliya's 13.866.

Once again Simone was in the lead, this time by a commanding 1.533 points (while that may seem like a small margin, it's a *huge* lead in gymnastics).

By the time she stood on the mat to start her floor routine as the last performer of the night, she knew gold was there for the taking. Aliya's overall score had even been passed by Aly Raisman, thanks to Aly's tremendous execution on a very difficult floor routine.

Aly Raisman was competing in her second Olympics after winning a gold medal in 2012. She was famous and a hero to gymnasts around the world. Yet she knew that she wasn't going to beat Simone's score. Simone's lead was so large, and her routine so challenging, she could fall multiple times and still win.

Aly was fine with that. She, along with everyone else in attendance, knew there really was no competing with Simone Biles.

"[US teammate] Laurie Hernandez said to me, 'If you get silver, you're the best because Simone doesn't count,'" Aly said with a laugh. "Her start value is [so much] higher than me so I know I can't beat her."

Simone didn't like that kind of talk—she wanted to encourage her teammates. She loved them and was proud of how good they were. "I get more excited when they win," she said. When Aly finished her brilliant floor routine to assure her at least a silver medal, she cried in delight, with Simone hugging and celebrating with her.

Suddenly Simone was fighting back tears of joy for Aly. "I thought, 'Oh my God, she's going to make me cry before my floor,'" Simone later said with a laugh. "And that wasn't going to be good."

With what felt like the whole world watching Simone, it was not the time to think of Aly or anyone else. This was about doing what she had trained to do. This was the time to concentrate. This was the time to win.

As the music started, the anxiety melted away and a huge smile broke out on her face.

"That is all we needed to see," her older brother, Adam, who was also there cheering her on, said. "As long as she has a smile on her face, we know she is in a good place."

Soon she was sprinting down the mat for her first tumbling run and springing into her round-off. Her muscles were trained. Her mind was clear.

"Sometimes nothing goes through my mind," Simone said. "When I tumble, I just tumble."

She soared nearly ten feet into the air before landing cleanly, with just a small hop to take away the momentum. The crowd roared. Soon she was repeating it . . . the buildup of speed, the concentration, the flying toward glory before ending with a sound, sharp landing.

Just like that, Simone Biles knew she was going to win gold.

"Once the first two passes were out of the way, I knew I was good," she said.

Everyone knew. The crowd was now on its collective feet, waving flags and roaring in delight. This was the ultimate performance, a dream combination of skill and entertainment. Simone leaping. Simone flipping. Simone in total command.

"The joy," Bela Karolyi said of watching it. "The satisfaction."

"Pride," her dad said.

This is what Simone wanted—to perform for the beauty of performing. Not for judges. Not for medals. She had always loved gymnastics for the sake of gymnastics. She hadn't reached the national team until she was fifteen, late for the great ones. No one had ever doubted her ability, but coaches were frustrated that she sometimes wanted gymnastics to be more about fun than just work.

Simone liked to smile at practice. She liked to laugh. "Gymnastics is supposed to be fun," she'd say.

Eventually her performances got so good and her technical ability so precise that even Martha Karolyi gave up trying to rein her in. Martha was a taskmaster. She was forever pushing gymnasts to be better and better. She wasn't much for laughs and smiles during training.

Simone, though . . . well, Simone could pretty much do whatever she wanted. The performance, and the results, spoke for her.

"Simone Biles is the biggest talent," Martha said. "Combined with the very good discipline of work and great preparation for consistency, she is the best."

By the time her routine ended, Simone was beaming. She rushed off the mat and hugged Coach Aimee, hugged Martha, and eventually wound up in a prolonged hug with Aly. Four years prior, she'd watched Aly win team gold for the Americans at the 2012 London Olympics. Simone considered Aly a role model.

At the time, there was no guarantee that Simone would ever make the senior national team, or World Championships, or these Olympics. She was fifteen and still hadn't broken through. Now four years later, there they were, the two of them awaiting the final scores.

When the scores were presented, the pair hugged even tighter. Simone had scored a 15.933 on floor, the highest score by any competitor in any event that night. That meant she won all-around gold over Aly by a whopping 2.100 margin.

The 2.1 differential wasn't just the largest margin of victory in the history of the Olympic women's all-around. It was larger than the combined margins of victory of every Olympic all-around, 1980–2012. By comparison, Gabby Douglas won all-around gold in 2012 by just 0.259.

Simone had blown out the competition. She would climb atop the podium and receive her medal, and yet even with all that she'd accomplished, she said she didn't feel a whole lot different.

"I'm still the same old Simone," she said.

The road to gold hadn't been easy. It had been full of twists and turns, laden with doubts and down periods.

She had made it, though. She had fulfilled her goal of reaching the Olympics.

There was also that goal she'd written down in her notebook.

"I will make you proud," she had promised her mother.

Up in the stands, with her parents and siblings crying tears of happiness, there was no doubt she had done that, too.

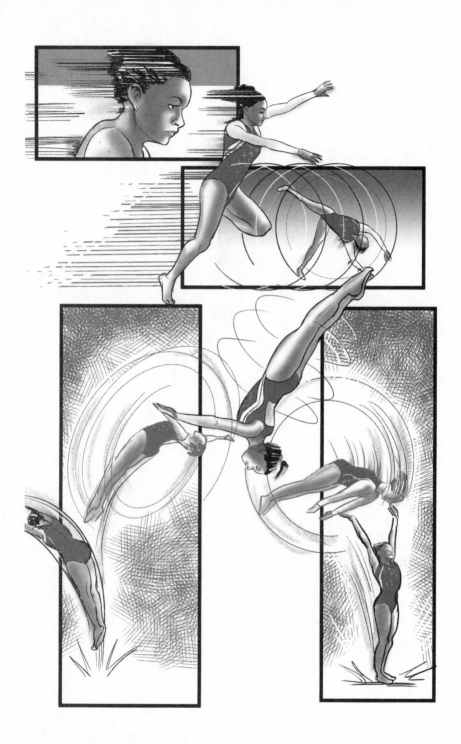

# 2
# Early Years

**S**IMONE ARIANNE BILES was born March 14, 1997, in Columbus, Ohio. She was the third child of her mother, Shanon Biles. She joined seven-year-old sister Ashley and three-year-old brother Tevin. Simone's younger sister, Adria, was born a couple of years later.

Simone's grandfather, Ron, had been a big fan of a popular singer from the 1960s named Nina Simone and always liked her last name. When Shanon wondered what to name her new daughter, Ron suggested Simone. Shanon agreed.

Simone's father, Kelvin Clemons, was part of neither her life nor her mother's life when she was born. Both her mother and father dealt with significant substance abuse issues. As a result, Simone's life was very unstable and chaotic. Meals were often skipped. Clothes were often dirty and worn. The family moved often, sometimes monthly. Money was extremely tight.

By the time Simone was three years old, a neighbor discovered her and her siblings playing unsupervised in the street. Shanon was nowhere to be found. The neighbor already suspected the children were often being left alone for long periods of time. In this case, the neighbor thought they were in danger, little kids running around with no one to watch them.

With no other option, the neighbor called child services and reported the situation. When officials investigated, they found the house and the circumstances unsuitable for young children to live in. Simone and her brother and sisters were taken off to foster care. Adria was just a baby, four months old.

"It was hard to give up my kids, but I had to do what I had to," Shanon told the *Daily Mail* newspaper years later. "I wasn't able to care for them."

A foster home is generally a local family that is willing to take care of kids who are being neglected. It is not a permanent solution. The families take the kids in and get them out of danger until either their biological parents can get their lives together or child services can find a family to adopt them. Often times the foster family already has children, either their own or adopted ones.

Simone and her siblings were placed in a foster home that provided the type of stability they'd lacked in their old home. Their foster parents, Mr. Leo and Miss Doris, were very nice. There were regular meals, including a home-cooked dinner every night. The home was clean and well cared for. At least one time Simone's foster parents took everyone camping, which Simone had never done before but found fun. Mostly it was safe. While Ashley and Tevin missed their old home, Simone was so young that she later said she wasn't really aware that she was missing anything.

There was one thing she didn't like. The family had a trampoline in the backyard, but the foster kids weren't allowed to use it because their foster parents worried about them getting injured. There are a lot of rules foster parents must follow, and keeping their kids physically safe is a big one. Simone was still very small, so a trampoline could be dangerous. She said later she would watch as other kids did flips on the trampoline and wish she could join in on the fun. She was certain she could jump higher than the other kids, even the older ones.

"I was already a fearless little tomboy," Simone wrote in the book, *Courage to Soar*.

Despite that restriction, Simone had a positive experience staying with Mr. Leo and Miss Doris. But foster care was a temporary living situation. She needed a permanent home she could grow up in, as Shanon continued to struggle with her addiction.

That's when a somewhat familiar face showed up at the door of Simone's foster home—her grandfather, the same one who'd helped choose her name.

Ron Biles lived outside Houston, Texas, with his wife, Nellie. He had grown up in Cleveland, Ohio. After high school, Ron joined the Air Force. For a while, he was stationed outside San Antonio and his daughter Shanon lived with him. But eventually, Shanon went to live with her mother, whom Ron had dated before meeting Nellie.

Ron tried to visit Shanon—and all her children (his grandchildren)—as often as possible. That included Simone, which is why she was excited to see him the day he arrived at her foster home. She knew her grandfather was a caring and loving man.

After the Air Force, Ron worked as an air traffic controller at an airport, where he'd help direct planes to take off and land, and then later was employed by a company that set up radar systems. He and Nellie had set up a sturdy and stable life in Texas, where they raised two boys, Ron II, who was sixteen at the time, and Adam, who was fourteen.

Child services had contacted Ron and told him that his grandchildren were in foster care and the situation with Shanon had deteriorated. He was told that the kids needed a dependable family to raise them and if a relative couldn't do it, then they might be split up in the foster system. He quickly flew to Ohio to investigate the situation and see if he could solve the problem.

He wanted Shanon to get sober and be a responsible mother. That wasn't happening, though, so he knew he and Nellie would have to step in. It was a very difficult decision. Their two boys were nearly grown, both in high school. They were getting older and weren't expecting to suddenly have to raise four more children, including a three-year-old (Simone) and a baby (Adria). Basically, their entire life was about to get turned upside down.

"I knew something had to be done," Ron said. "I knew I couldn't let these kids get split up."

He and Nellie agreed to take all four of the children in. Their home in Texas would be crowded and money would be stretched thin, but they hoped it would be temporary until Shanon straightened her life out. Their home had always been filled with love and support, so while the decision was difficult and unexpected, they knew it was for the best. Some of Nellie's friends even threw her a "baby shower" like she was a new mother, because the family suddenly needed lots of supplies and toys for young children and diapers and bottles for the baby.

When the kids flew to Texas they found a home far nicer than what they were used to. Ron and Nellie weren't considered wealthy, but life with Shanon had been poor and chaotic. Simone, Ashley, and Adria would share a room. Tevin would move in with Adam. There were new clothes, books to read, and a garage full of bicycles and scooters.

Best of all, there was a trampoline in the backyard that Simone could finally use. She would go out there every day and jump and flip to her heart's delight. Some days, Ron and Nellie had to drag her off the trampoline to come in for dinner or bedtime. It seemed like all Simone wanted to do was bounce.

As much as the new home was fun and exciting, it came with an equal dose of discipline and responsibility. Nellie believed in everyone helping with chores, even little Simone. Vegetables and meat, which Simone didn't like at the time, had to be eaten during sit-down dinners. Table manners had to be honored. And bedtime meant *bedtime*. It wasn't always easy, but Simone understood the trade-off was worth it.

Shanon kept calling Ron and Nellie, asking to come and see her children. She loved the kids, but she struggled to live a sober life and act as a responsible adult. Eventually, Ron and Nellie relented. The older kids, Ashley and Tevin, had spent more time with their mother and were excited when she came. Simone and Adria were so young that they were already more attached to their grandparents. This was home to them.

Shanon wanted all the kids to come back to Columbus, Ohio, with her, and it became a big debate in the family on what to do. Life was better in Texas, but the house was crowded, and having four new children put a great strain on Ron and Nellie. The situation was uncertain.

As the kids' mother, Shanon had legal control. For a while, all four kids moved back to Ohio and lived again with their original foster family. That was supposed to be temporary. Child services wouldn't allow Shanon to regain full custody until she passed a series of drug tests. Shanon kept failing the tests, though.

Eventually, child services ruled that she wasn't allowed to get the kids back.

As a result, it was decided that Ashley and Tevin would go and live with an aunt in the Cleveland area. Simone and Adria would return to Texas and live with Ron and Nellie. Shanon would continue to work on getting sober.

Simone was five when she returned to Spring, Texas, to live with her grandparents. They didn't just want to be her grandparents anymore, though. They wanted to be Simone and Adria's actual parents. Shanon had been persuaded to give up her parental rights since she wasn't capable of raising the children. It was a very tough decision, but she did it for the good of her kids.

She slowly rebuilt her life and says she has been

sober since 2007. She still calls Simone on birthdays and holidays, but for many years they had no contact because Ron and Nellie thought it would be unfair and confusing to the girls.

"I didn't understand it at the time," Shanon told the *Daily Mail*. "But years later, I understood why. I had to deal with me first."

Almost immediately, Ron and Nellie began the process of adopting Simone and Adria and legally becoming their parents. That way, the girls would be safe with them and neither child services nor Shanon could have any control over them. For Simone and Adria, moving back and forth and never knowing what was coming next had been hard. Now everything would be settled as they grew up.

On November 7, 2003, everyone dressed up and went down to a local courthouse in Harris County, Texas. Simone was six. Adria was three. A few minutes later, Ron and Nellie Biles were no longer Simone and Adria's grandfather and grandmother.

They were Mom and Dad.

# 3

# Bouncy

**O**N FALL SUNDAY AFTERNOONS, Ron Biles loved nothing more than settling into his chair in the living room to watch football games on TV.

Yet suddenly it wasn't very relaxing anymore. Every time Ron sat down for a game and tried to focus on the action, he said his daughter Simone would come flying by. Literally, flying. She'd do cartwheels through the room, or crash into the couch, or use the end table as a way to spring into the air. She was just four, five, six years old, but she was already a complete ball of energy. Little sister Adria was usually twirling right behind her.

"Simone was bouncy and loud," Ron said. "She was just a bouncy child, jumping all over the place, messing up the furniture. I'd be trying to watch football and they'd be making noise, jumping around."

Ron didn't know anything about gymnastics. He had a sense that his daughters, Simone in particular, were pretty athletic, but he didn't pay much attention to the sport.

Nellie, meanwhile, had grown up in Belize, a small country in Central America. Gymnastics wasn't popular there, so she also knew nothing about it beyond the fact that it was an Olympic sport. The idea of sending their kids to train in gymnastics had never dawned on the couple.

Ron did think it might be a good idea to get them involved in a sport, though, if only to burn off extra energy.

"I didn't know what we needed to do," he said, laughing at the memory. "But I knew we needed to do something. They were going to knock over the house."

At the time, Simone and Adria were enrolled in a local day care. Simone's older brother Adam was working at the day care center while attending a local college. One day a field trip to a farm was scheduled, but it was raining. Rather than be cooped up inside all day, they went to a local gymnastics hall called Bannon's Gymnastix.

The moment Simone walked into Bannon's Gymnastix she knew she was home.

There were mats and equipment and bars to swing on and padding everywhere. Unlike her parents' living room, this was a place that encouraged people to jump and flip and twist and go as wild as they wanted. She was in heaven.

Soon Adam and Simone were on a mat when Adam attempted to do a flip. He almost landed it, but wound up falling awkwardly. Simone laughed. If it was so easy, Adam told his little sister, then you do it.

So Simone did it, leaping up, flipping in the air, and landing cleanly on her feet. Then she did it again, adding a twist before sticking the landing. It was effortless, almost too easy to believe. Most kids have to spend months or even years perfecting the form and building the strength necessary to complete a flip. For Simone, it was just something she'd learned to do on that trampoline in her parents' backyard.

Just then, a woman who had been working the

front desk came over. Her name was Veronica and, according to *Courage to Soar*, she had a question for Adam.

"Has she had any formal gymnastics training?" Veronica asked.

"No," Adam said.

Veronica was a bit stunned that someone with no training could be so good. She sent Simone home with a flyer that contained information about Bannon's Gymnastix's recreational classes.

Simone's mother quickly signed up both Simone and Adria. She didn't envision it being anything more than a way for her extremely active kids to play in a safe environment.

The classes were basic. The teachers tried to maintain order and show the kids some fundamental skills, but not all of them took it seriously. It was just supposed to be fun. No one thought there might be a future Olympic champion in the class. For her part, Simone was excited that her mother had bought her a shiny leotard in Bannon's store.

Right away, though, the coach of the rec class noticed Simone. How couldn't she? Simone stood out immediately. She was only six and very small, even for her age, but she had actual muscles and was clearly a natural athlete. Mostly she couldn't sit still. She was just all energy. The coach had been involved in gymnastics for decades and had seen thousands of young gymnasts. Kids like Simone just don't come around every day.

The coach felt Simone had a future at more competitive levels of gymnastics. She couldn't have imagined that six-year-old Simone would one day make the Olympics, but she believed the high school level was a possibility.

Bannon's had a higher level of training than their rec class, which was called the USA Gymnastics Junior Olympic (JO) program. Kids would learn and proceed through the ten skill levels as determined by USA Gymnastics (USAG). The early levels are fairly basic and are generally for beginners. To pass Level 1, for example, a kid only needs to be able to do a three-quarter handstand, cartwheel, backward roll, forward roll, and a split jump with 30-degree leg separation.

The degree of skill and talent needed grows with each level. Gymnasts aren't even allowed to attempt Level 10 until they are nine years old, and only a small number ever reach that stage. To progress requires lots and lots of training and eventually competition going from district to state, then regional and eventually national, if someone makes it that far.

Within a week or so, Simone caught the eye of Aimee Boorman, who was a higher-level coach who taught competition gymnasts at Bannon's. Aimee didn't usually pay attention to the rec classes, but there was no way to miss Simone. Sensing Simone's natural talent, Aimee watched closely and quickly moved Simone into the JO program.

For Simone, the positive reinforcement of having coaches notice her and take an interest in her was important. She realized that she was, indeed, good at gymnastics. She also understood there was a long way to go. But here were these coaches willing to bring her along, teach her new skills, and make her better.

For a kid who was happy just jumping on the backyard trampoline, this was incredible. Aimee asked if she wanted to come to Bannon's more often and train for longer periods of time.

Of course, Simone said. Of course she did. She couldn't get enough. She begged her parents to start dropping her off at the gym nearly every day.

"She's been there ever since," Ron Biles said.

★ ★ ★

Simone had almost everything a kid could want growing up. The family wasn't necessarily rich, but they didn't lack for anything either. They had a nice home with a nice yard in a nice neighborhood. Her parents were loving and supportive. It was everything a kid could want.

Well, there was one thing they didn't have . . . a dog.

Simone and Adria wanted one, preferably a small, cute dog such as a Yorkie or a Chihuahua. They loved playing with their friends' dogs and their neighbors' dogs and any dog they ran into at the park. They were obsessed with getting a dog.

The problem? Their parents did not want a dog. Dealing with all these kids and all these busy schedules was enough. There was work and school and all sorts of responsibilities.

Simone's dad figured that if they got a dog, the girls would care for it for a couple of weeks or months, but soon enough he'd end up being the one walking the dog, training it, and cleaning up after it. He thought the family was just too busy to add any pets.

One year, for Christmas, he bought both girls big-dog stuffed animals, put them under the tree, and declared that the family now had two dogs.

The girls liked the stuffed animals and enjoyed their dad's humor, but that wasn't enough. It certainly didn't stop them from asking and asking, hoping that they might eventually wear their parents down.

Finally, when Simone was eleven, there was a crack in the resistance to getting a dog.

By that time, Simone had been quickly rising up the rungs of the USAG skill levels. Simone was scheduled to compete in the Region 3 Championships, a Level 9 meet. It was a big-time event for her. If she did well enough, she would qualify for the Western Championships in St. Charles, Missouri, just outside St. Louis. The Westerns were an even bigger event, with many of the best gymnasts from around the country competing.

Also in attendance would be the top coaches from USA Gymnastics, including the national team director, Martha Karolyi, and her husband, Bela.

The Karolyis were originally from Romania and considered the best gymnastics coaches in the world. Back in the 1970s, when Bela had been in charge of the Romanian national team, he built a system that focused on fundamentals and regimented training. He began developing some of the top teams and individual gymnasts of all time.

That included Nadia Comăneci. At the 1976 Olympics, Nadia was just fourteen years old, but she won three gold medals, secured seven "Perfect 10" scores (the sport had a different scoring system then), and mesmerized the world with her performances.

She became a hero to people around the world, particularly young girls who saw her as a role model. Gymnastics wasn't nearly as popular then as it is now, but millions watched the Olympics on television. Nadia was so brilliant that she inspired a generation of young American athletes even though she wasn't from America. At the 1980 Olympics, she returned to win two more golds and two silvers. She remains one of the most famous and beloved gymnasts ever.

In 1981 the Karolyis immigrated to the United States and immediately attracted some top talent desperate to work with "Nadia's coach."

At the 1984 Olympics, Bela coached Mary Lou Retton, who hailed from West Virginia and became the first American to ever win an all-around gold medal. She was considered an American hero and starred in television commercials and shows. As a result, gymnastics halls and training sessions began popping up in nearly every community in America, as kids begged their parents to let them try the sport.

Gymnastics, which for years had been dominated by Russia and other eastern European countries, now had a new contender—the United States.

Through the years, Bela continued coaching many of the best American gymnasts, racking up Olympic medals and World Championships.

At the 1996 Olympics, he was the personal coach of two members of Team USA's so-called "Magnificent Seven," who were battling to become the first Americans to win a team Olympic gold medal.

One of them, Kerri Strug, injured her ankle on her first vault during the team competition. She tried to shake off the injury, but it appeared as if she might not be able to attempt a required second vault. But Bela believed in her and kept pushing her to try.

Full of nerves and adrenaline, Kerri attempted the second vault and miraculously landed it cleanly, mostly on just one leg! It clinched the gold for the Americans and the video of the triumphant moment continues to be replayed to this day. Afterward, Bela carried Kerri to the medal stand, and a photo of the pair was taken that has proven iconic. He was more famous than ever.

Simone, like almost every gymnast, had seen the

photo with Kerri Strug and watched Nadia's performances on YouTube. She knew who the Karolyis were. She knew that while Aimee would remain her individual coach, to have the Karolyis, as national team directors, also coach her was the opportunity of a lifetime.

They were, to put it simply, gymnastics legends.

"The chance to be coached by the Karolyis was everything," Simone said. "It's all anyone ever wanted. You knew they coached all of these champions, so for them to work with you just meant so much."

Not only were the Karolyis the best coaches in the world, they had final say on who did or didn't make the senior United States national team that competes in the Olympics and the World Championships. They even owned and operated a gymnastics center outside Huntsville, Texas. It was known as the Karolyi Ranch and beginning in the early 2000s, it served as a place for the girls on the national team to come for intensive training sessions about once a month.

Every gymnast at that time knew that to ever make it really big in the sport, they needed to impress the Karolyis and get to the Karolyi Ranch. But first they needed to make sure the Karolyis even knew their name. Making the Western Championships was Simone's first opportunity to do that.

Which is how the entire "getting-a-dog" thing came into play.

Simone's parents were mostly hands-off when it came to gymnastics. Her mother would drop her off at Bannon's and then come back a few hours later and pick her up. She rarely stayed to watch practice. Her dad would come to meets, but he was busy working and taking care of the other kids. They loved that she loved gymnastics, but they didn't want to make a big deal out of it when it was just supposed to be pure enjoyment for the kids. Gymnastics wasn't their life.

"Nothing was planned," Simone's dad said of her growth as a gymnast. "She had the opportunity to go to the gym, enjoyed it. We didn't know where it would lead her. We just wanted her to have fun and be the best she could be every day. We never wanted to pressure her."

The Biles family was all about academics. They were relentless at monitoring the girls' progress in school and wanted them to attend college. Any slip-up with a grade was taken very seriously. Chores around the house were mandatory. Discipline was maintained at all times.

"My parents were so strict," Simone said.

They were also very protective of their kids. They didn't believe in sleepovers with friends or trips to the mall or wandering off without adult supervision, even in their own safe neighborhood. They'd seen how bad decisions, drugs, and alcohol could affect young people. They were determined to make sure the girls reached their potential.

The Biles family spent their time focused on that. Gymnastics kept Simone busy. That she was really good at it was just a bonus.

Except even Ron Biles knew how important it was for eleven-year-old Simone to qualify for Westerns and get a chance to compete in front of the Karolyis. Anyone who knew anything about gymnastics understood that.

So he made Simone a deal in an effort to provide just a little extra motivation at the Region 3 Championships.

"Okay, Simone," Ron Biles said, according to *Courage to Soar.* "I'll tell you what. You qualify for Westerns this year, you'll get your dog."

"Are you serious?" Simone said in disbelief.

There was one catch. The dog would be a German shepherd, not some cute little dog. Ron didn't want a small dog. Simone and Adria didn't care. A dog was a dog. Simone had already been focused and motivated for Region 3 Championships, but now she was somehow even *more* focused and motivated. This was her chance. And Adria kept reminding her not to blow it.

With her parents and Adria watching from the stands, and a dog on the line, Simone stepped onto the mat at the Region 3 Championships. With the pressure on, she finished first on the floor and second all-around, with a score of 38.100. It was enough to qualify for Westerns.

More important, Simone had won her dog. Adria cheered in delight for what her sister had done for them.

Soon enough, the Biles family went to a farm that raised German shepherds, and there at the end of a line of cages Simone saw a black-and-brown puppy. She named her Maggie Elena Biles and just like that, her career was moving to the national level, and she had a cute dog at home to play with.

# 4

# Development

**T**HE GOOD NEWS for Simone was that she didn't just get one dog. In the years to come Maggie Elena Biles gave birth to puppies, three of whom—Atlas, Bella, and Lily—lived with the Bileses. A house that once had no dogs was suddenly overrun with them.

The bad news? Simone didn't overly impress the Karolyis or any of the other USA Gymnastics coaches at the 2008 Western Championships. She finished tied for 16th overall, a full 1.075 behind the winner. She was tied for 4th on vault and 8th on floor, but she was a dismal 24th on bars and 33rd on beam. She was not getting invited to the Karolyi Ranch with that performance.

The scores reflected Simone as a gymnast at the time. She was an incredible athlete and a powerful tumbler. But to be a full gymnast, to truly master the sport, she needed to be more precise in every movement in every discipline.

She might be able to fly high enough to deliver on floor and vault, but bars called for an almost completely different skill set, and beam was unforgiving to even the slightest lapse in concentration. There were times that Simone was *too* athletic and *too* strong for the beam because it could push or pull her off balance. On the floor or vault, she was capable of recovering. On beam and bars, she couldn't.

There was no question Simone was a talented prospect. She wasn't truly elite yet, though. She needed to get to Level 10 and then begin excelling in individual meets.

The Bileses moved before Simone was about to enter 8th grade. Their new house was bigger, allowing both Simone and Adria to have their own rooms. It even had a pool. Simone loved it.

Rather than start her at a new public school near her new home, the Bileses enrolled Simone in a private school located across the street from Bannon's

Gymnastix. Simone wanted to increase the amount of time she spent training. This way, she could get dropped off at Bannon's at seven a.m., work out until nine, and then walk to her new school. At the end of the school day, she'd walk back for a second training session. This allowed her to jump from twenty hours a week in the gym to thirty hours a week.

Throughout 2009 and 2010, Simone continued to improve, placing well in a series of meets, most of them in the Houston area. She finished first all-around at the Space City Classic, the Ricky Deci Invitational, and the New Orleans Jazz Invitational.

Yet her first-place finishes were often a result of racking up huge scores on vault and floor that allowed her to overcome not being 100 percent sound on beam and, especially, bars. That wasn't good enough to take her to the next level. It wasn't just her performance. Her degree of difficulty in those events wasn't up to the same standard as her competitors.

Still, around Simone's thirteenth birthday, Aimee decided to send video of Simone's performances to Martha and Bela Karolyi in the hope they would see her potential and invite her to train once a month at their camp. Martha wasn't impressed, though.

"This kid has no bars," Martha told Aimee, according to *Courage to Soar*. "I can't let her come to camp. She can tumble great, but that's it."

It was tough for Simone to hear. She was a good gymnast and one who was on pace to earn a scholarship and be a major talent at the collegiate level. Her dreams, however, had grown much larger by that point. Now she had her sights set on the Olympics, the World Championships, the chance to be among the four or five best in the country, if not the world.

Thirteen isn't very old, but in top-level gymnastics, most of the best competitors have established themselves by that age. Simone hadn't. And she wasn't getting any younger. At the 2010 Houston National Invitational, a major event in which Simone finished third in the Junior A division, another soon-to-be-thirteen-year-old Texan named Madison Kocian won the top open division. That's where Simone needed to be.

Simone, her parents, and Aimee had a long talk and tried to come up with a plan that would close the gap. The key, they believed, was making a major jump in degree of difficulty and then challenging Simone to perfect it. That meant daring and difficult routines, especially on bars, where Simone sometimes struggled. The next year, they believed, was make or break. Simone would either excel and move on to the elite national levels or plateau and be a great college gymnast, which was certainly nothing to feel bad about.

Although some saw Simone as a late bloomer, she was never discouraged. Mostly she loved going to the gym every day, even as the training got harder and harder and Aimee got more and more demanding. As long as she was having fun and progress was being made, then she still believed she could be an Olympian.

In 2011, that breakthrough finally came. Simone won the all-around title at the Metroplex Challenge in Fort Worth, Texas. She then traveled to Riverside, California, for the Gliders National Elite Qualifier, her first truly big elite junior meet. At the time, she was still mostly unknown, this short fourteen-year-old from Houston with a lot of potential.

She also stood out because of her race. Even though there'd been other prominent African American gymnasts in the past—Dianne Durham and Luci Collins in the 1980s, Dominique Dawes at the 1996 Olympics—the sport was still mostly white. That was slowly changing, of course. Gabby Douglas was set to make the 2012 Olympic team and went on to become the first African American to win all-around gold. Still, this was not a sport of great diversity.

Simone understood that. She just rejected letting herself be labeled like that. In the future, there would be people who rooted for Simone in part because she was African American and thus a source of pride for their community. However, Simone was uncomfortable receiving attention for that. She was a gymnast, not a black gymnast. She was Simone. That's who she wanted to be known as.

"Plain and simple she doesn't do anything about the color of her skin," Aimee said. "People like to make it like that, but she doesn't. That's just how her whole family is."

Indeed, Ron and Nellie Biles wanted their kids to focus on things they could control. How good a student they could be. The effort level they put into tasks. The kindness with which they approached the world.

"She's a caring, humble person," Simone's dad said. "That is what matters. She cares about the family and life and she enjoys life."

Ignoring the potential distractions, Simone showed she was more than just a tumbler by finishing first on vault *and* beam at Gliders. She added a third place finish on floor and a fifth on uneven bars to win the all-around title.

It was the performance that Simone had been waiting for. Not only did she show she could be a force on the national elite junior level, but the victory qualified her for the American Classic, which would be held in July 2011 at the Karolyi Ranch. If she did well enough there, she would get to compete at the Visa Championships, where the junior national team would be selected.

At last Simone would be able to show the Karolyis what she was made of.

But Aimee felt there was no need to wait for the American Classic. Once again, she sent video of Simone's performances to Martha Karolyi. Martha analyzed the Gliders tape and was impressed. She invited Simone to a developmental camp. Simone had clearly put in the work and honed her skills just as Martha had wanted.

Yes, she was fourteen, which was old to "finally" arrive at this level. And yes, due to her "advanced" age, Martha wasn't sure how much more growth was possible. But there was clearly something special here. Now it was on Simone to prove it.

She was just excited. She was headed to the Karolyi Ranch. At last.

# 5

# The Ranch

IN 1983, BELA KAROLYI bought 40 acres in the woods near Huntsville, Texas. Over the years he cleared some of the trees and built a state-of-the-art gymnastics training center designed to attract the best gymnasts from around the country, and even the world.

The Karolyi Ranch, or just "the Ranch," as it came to be known, is a gymnast's paradise. There are three modern gyms, with rows of balance beams and uneven bars. There are dormitories that sleep up to 300 people—gymnasts, their personal coaches, and support staff. There is a cafeteria, medical facilities, and even tennis courts and a swimming pool.

This was the Karolyis' base of operation, where they began coaching Olympic and World Champions, including, almost immediately, Mary Lou Retton. By 2000, USA Gymnastics deemed it the official National Team Training Center.

With hiking trails, a lake in the middle, and terms such as "Ranch" and "Camp" getting thrown around, it might sound like a relaxing and fun environment. It isn't. This is a place of incredible intensity, demands, and expectations.

"The girls go there to train," Martha said. "That is the only reason."

Top gymnasts have traveled from all over the world to get to the Ranch, but for Simone the trip was just an hour's ride from her house. Aimee drove her up, the two of them a mix of excitement and nerves.

The system the Karolyis created called for gymnasts to continue training with their individual coaches, but with Martha, the national team coordinator, overseeing everything. So Aimee was still Simone's coach, but Martha was also present, watching their every move.

The five-day developmental camp was designed to take elite gymnasts to the next level. Training went from eight in the morning until about noon and then restarted around three and ran to seven at night. The Karolyis' approach was all about repetition in pursuit of perfection.

The slightest flaws were picked apart. There were no easy reps or weak efforts. You didn't spend time laughing and joking with the other gymnasts. It was a complete grind, both physically and mentally—all with Martha Karolyi, the woman who picks the national team, wandering about and shouting directions.

Martha was an intimidating figure. Always with her hair perfect and wearing makeup, she spoke with a thick eastern European accent. If she was happy, you knew it. If she wasn't, you also knew it—and you'd better step lightly. Her goal wasn't to make the gymnasts happy, but to push and push and push. If nothing else, by her bringing many top gymnasts together, they could see how strong their competition was and get motivated to work even harder.

"A healthy competition is always very good," Martha said. "Certainly it brings the level higher and higher."

The Karoylis believed that there were many talented gymnasts in the world. But mental toughness, even more than skill, is what determines who wins medals and who doesn't. The goal was to demand excellence and create a team that was mentally and emotionally hardened and ready to compete.

This was no longer just some fun sport to play. Every minute of every day was about eventually defeating the Russians or Chinese in international meets. If you wanted anything less than that, well, there were a thousand other girls dying to come and take your place.

"The atmosphere was more hard-core than I was used to at Bannon's," Simone wrote in *Courage to Soar*. "Martha is very no-nonsense, and she wants results fast . . . She'll push you to limits that you don't think you can reach, and yet somehow you do. She definitely wants you to be your best, so I knew everything we were doing at camp was going to make me better.

"But I wasn't used to such a serious environment," Simone continued. "Even when hard practices made me cry at Bannon's, some other part of that session would make me break into laughter. It's just who I am. But I had to keep that side of me tamped down because laughter in the gym would've been seen as a sign I wasn't committed. At the Ranch, being committed meant you kept a straight face and did the conditioning and worked at perfecting your skills until you thought you were so tired you couldn't go on—and then you worked some more."

Needless to say, this was not Simone's preferred style of training.

"Simone is definitely a giggly girl," Martha said.

The five-day camp featured thirty girls and it's possible that Simone was the most miserable of them all. She became frustrated with the drills and the relentlessness required. Simone had worked hard and been pushed hard and trained hard. You didn't get to her level any other way. But the challenge the Ranch posed was on a different wavelength entirely.

"One of the things with Simone is, she is definitely the type of athlete where if you made her do a lot of hours with a lot of repetition she [might say], 'This isn't any fun. I quit. I'll go run track,'" Aimee said.

The camp was built to weed out those gymnasts who couldn't withstand the pressure. Martha believed it was best to push their limits now rather than have a gymnast quit in the middle of an Olympic competition and impact the team. The Karolyis had a track record of success that spanned decades. Their system worked. The gymnasts would have to adapt or give up.

Aimee had to keep pushing Simone and reminding her this is what it took. There was a reason that some of the girls were at levels above Simone, and it wasn't a lack of talent.

"Up until then, gymnastics had been mostly fun and games for me," Simone wrote. "I had to start seeing it as work too."

Simone didn't quit. She worked harder and harder. When camp ended, she felt she had learned a lot and shown she could hang with the best. She had certainly gotten the attention of the most important person at the camp . . . Martha.

"Simone had a real special talent," Martha said. "The first time I saw her, what stood out was that she was extremely bouncy. She was a very talented tumbler."

Now she had to prove she could be an all-around gymnast. A few weeks later, on July 1, Simone returned to the Ranch to compete in the American Classic. This was an important event, and not just because it was the first since camp. If Simone scored high enough, she could qualify for the Visa Championships in August, where a strong performance could land her a spot on the junior national team.

There were just 35 competitors, 11 of them "seniors" and 24 of them "juniors" who would be divided into two sessions. Simone, due to her age (fourteen) and level of previous success, was a junior.

The camp had clearly improved her skills. Her routines were sharper, which made her more confident. She was also more familiar with the national stage—she had befriended a number of the other junior competitors during downtime at the camp. The grueling nature of the camp had actually brought them closer together—another goal for the Karolyis, who felt that gymnasts compete better when there are friendships and team support.

As she returned to the Ranch, Simone felt she belonged.

And then she proved it. She finished first on vault, first on beam, and third overall. She was ecstatic.

She now understood completely why the Karolyis were so demanding and why their camps were so difficult. She had made an enormous leap as a gymnast in just five days. The grind of camp had brought the best out of her, and while she might never truly like the intensity of those national camps, she'd never again wonder if they were worth it.

"Martha has this talent for getting the last two percent out of an athlete," Aimee told *Texas Monthly* magazine. "She can bring Simone to that level of polish that I can't necessarily get day to day. At camp, they all stand a little taller. They're all a little more bright-eyed. They all want her approval."

Simone's score of 53.650 easily qualified her for the National Championships.

Her chance of reaching the junior national team, the stepping-stone to the Olympic Games and World Championships, was next.

# 6

# Nationals

IN 1976, A THIRTEEN-YEAR-OLD GIRL from Canada named Karen Kelsall competed at the Olympics. Over the years, the sport grew more and more competitive and physically demanding. Gymnasts just kept inventing new and more dangerous moves. As such, the international governing body began increasing the age minimum for the highest competition in an effort to protect young gymnasts.

Since 1997, to be eligible for the Olympics, a gymnast has to either be sixteen or turning sixteen in that calendar year. This was bad luck for Simone.

She was born in 1997, and would turn fifteen in 2012, when the Olympics were set to be staged in London. There was nothing she could do, no score she could achieve, that would allow her to be an Olympian that year.

Simone would be able to compete in the annual World Championships starting in 2013, at age sixteen. For the Olympics, the biggest event of them all, she would have to wait until 2016, when she would be nineteen years old. The Summer Olympics are held just once every four years. For elite gymnasts, that can be considered old. Many of the all-time greats peaked at age sixteen or seventeen.

With the circumstances out of her control, Simone focused on making the national junior team in 2011. To be fair, she likely wasn't ready yet for the senior national team anyway. Making any national team would be an incredible accomplishment.

One of the barriers to fulfilling that dream was her degrees of difficulty on the beam and, especially, the uneven bars. Since judges tally a score on more than just how cleanly or perfectly a gymnast performs a certain move, a difficult move like a beam dismount of a flip with a twist is going to score more points than a simple round-off.

Martha had made it clear that Simone needed challenging routines to reach the national team. Aimee and her coaches at Bannon's were pushing Simone in that direction, especially on bars, where Simone had always struggled to get fully comfortable, even with relatively simple giant swings or dismounts.

One of the moves was Tkatchev, which was named after the Russian gymnast Alexander Tkatchev, who was the first to perform it in competition back in the 1970s. Most gymnastics moves are named after the athlete who first completed it.

On the Tkatchev, a gymnast must perform a giant swing on the high bar but as she approaches being vertical to the ground—or twelve o'clock—she lets go of the bar, flies over the bar backward, and then grabs the bar again as she begins to come down. For the truly elite gymnast, it isn't especially complicated. However, doing it the first time requires a lot of courage.

While first trying the move in practice, Simone had failed to regrab the bar and it became a mental hurdle she couldn't overcome. It felt like every time she tried the Tkatchev, she wound up falling off the bars and onto the mats at Bannon's. A coach would pick her up and she'd try again. Sometimes she'd make it, but not with the consistency that gave her confidence.

Then there was the Amanar (named after Romania's Simona Amânar), which is performed on the vault. Simone was already strong in that discipline, but Martha wanted her to become stronger. The Amanar called for a round-off entry (basically a cartwheel where you land on both feet at the same time) onto the springboard and then a two-and-a-half with a twist flip. It was an extremely challenging, world-class-level vault. But, as Martha said, world class is the standard for elite American gymnasts.

Simone worked on both maneuvers leading into the National Championships, but she wasn't confident in either one. On the vault, she preferred the Yurchenko, which calls for a round-off onto the springboard, then a back handspring onto the vault, and then a double-twisting layout into the landing. Simone could do that in her sleep. The Amanar was different.

"I'm not ready," Simone kept telling Aimee.

This is how it is for every gymnast at every level, from little kids dismounting or doing a simple vault, to the best of all time trying to add another rotation or twist to an already difficult maneuver. The sport never stops growing. To advance at any level, a gymnast needs to overcome doubt and fear, and persevere. If not, they watch their competition do it and leave them in the dust.

Being too courageous, however, can lead to injuries, sometimes serious ones that will set an athlete back.

In a sport that is often about balance, this is the greatest danger.

The 2011 National Championships were held in St. Paul, Minnesota, on August 18 and 20. This was everything Simone had long worked for, dreamed of, and, indeed, prayed to happen. The arena was huge—it's home to the Minnesota Wild of the National Hockey League and can seat nearly eighteen thousand fans. The lights were bright and the event would be televised nationally.

Simone was in the junior division, but there were also many of the best and most famous current senior gymnasts there—including past and future Olympians such as Shawn Johnson, Gabby Douglas, Aly Raisman, McKayla Maroney, Chellsie Memmel, and Jordyn Wieber, who would win the senior all-around title that weekend.

This was the big-time. It was easy to get overwhelmed, starstruck, and begin to believe that you don't belong. Simone was just a small kid from Bannon's Gymnastix, which, unlike some gyms, didn't have a tradition of churning out Olympians.

She desperately wanted to make the junior national team, but to do that she needed to finish in the top 13 against the toughest competition she'd ever faced.

Simone later acknowledged she lacked some belief in herself—"this lack of confidence messed with my head," she wrote. On the first day she performed well, though. She ranked 17th in all-around, powered mostly by finishing third in vault. The problem? She didn't perform the Amanar. Instead she stayed with the Yurchenko.

While Simone hit it nearly perfectly and her score of 14.900 was very good, she may have left valuable points on the table due to the lesser degree of difficulty. She knew that she needed vault, her best event, to rack up extra points and make up for some of her weaker ones, mostly the uneven bars, in which she finished 22nd.

Day two of the event was no different. Simone was terrific on beam (10th overall) and floor (12th overall) and struggled on bars (22nd overall). On vault, her chance to shine, she again failed to push for the Amanar as Martha wanted. She wound up wobbly on her landing anyway. Her score of 14.500 was a 1.4 behind the leader that day. For the entire event, Simone wound up 7th overall in vault.

As the final rotation was completed, Simone could only stand on the floor of the arena and look up at a giant scoreboard that slowly listed off the results. She felt regret and disappointment as much as worry. She believed she was one of the top 13 gymnasts there. She just wasn't sure she had proven it.

"I felt, deep down, that I could've done better," Simone wrote. "Maybe if I'd trained more, spent longer hours practicing in the gym, mastered more challenging skills—like the Amanar—I might [have felt] less scared."

Katelyn Ohashi finished number 1. Then came Kyla Ross at number 2. And so on and on. Finally it got to number 13, the final available spot for national team. The name flashed on the board . . . "Madison Desch."

Simone came next, 14th place. She had missed out by one spot, and just 0.800 points over two days of competition. She was crushed. She thought she failed.

Not doing the Amanar had cost her.

Aimee, her family, and everyone back at Bannon's were proud of how she had represented them and tried to cheer her up, telling her she would get them next time. But deep down Simone thought this was the end.

In reality, it was just the beginning.

# 7
# Soaring

**F**AILING TO MAKE THE 2011 junior national team made Simone question everything. Was she good enough? Was she training long enough? Was Aimee the right coach for her? Was this even something she truly wanted?

Back in Texas, Simone and Aimee sat down and watched the television footage from the competition. It was clear to them that the girls who made the team weren't necessarily better than Simone, they were simply more confident. It was that confidence that allowed them to perform more challenging skills, which racked them up extra points.

Yet that confidence could only come through extra work, repeating the routine so many times it becomes natural.

"The great ones are mentally tough and confident," Martha said. "The scoring system is about counting the difficulty level. The higher the difficulty, the more points you are able to collect. And then you have an execution score, which rewards how perfectly you have done. [A gymnast] has to believe they can do it."

Simone wasn't there yet. If she were to ever reach that level, she first had to ask herself: Did she even want to get there? It wasn't an easy question.

She was already talented enough that she could have a great career as a gymnast and earn a college scholarship—which had been a longtime goal of hers. To chase a spot on the national team, let alone winning Olympic medals, required much greater commitment.

To achieve the level of mental toughness that Martha described, Simone would need to up her training from around twenty-five to thirty hours a week to about thirty-five to forty hours a week.

She'd have to attend camps at the Karolyi Ranch on a near-monthly basis. She would have to be completely focused on improvement.

That meant she would need to be homeschooled. This would allow the academic schedule to be built around her schedule, rather than attend a normal high school, which was set to begin in a matter of days. Almost every elite gymnast was homeschooled. It was about the only way.

Simone had been excited for high school, though. She wanted to be around lots of kids her age, have friends, attend football games and dances. The decision was difficult. Was she willing to give up a normal teenage existence for gymnastics?

In the end she decided she wanted to be great. She wanted to keep going.

It wouldn't be easy. Training became grueling, six days a week, six to seven hours a day. There were routines performed over and over again. Exhausting conditioning sessions. Workout regimens consisting of sit-ups, crunches, and running up and down stairs. Aimee became a taskmaster, trying to push Simone to greater and greater heights. There were also more fees to pay for the increased training, which put the entire family under additional stress.

All the while, Simone was missing out on a normal high school life.

"Who is the best trained," Bela Karolyi said. "That is who wins."

In 2012, Simone drew motivation watching the Olympics. The United States team (featuring Gabby Douglas, Aly Raisman, McKayla Maroney, Jordyn Wieber, and Kyla Ross) won team gold. Gabby won all-around gold and Aly won gold on floor. McKayla brought home a silver on vault. They were dubbed the "Fierce Five" and were celebrated across the country for their excellence.

Far from the spotlight, Simone worked to reach their level. She knew there was no way to ever make the 2016 Olympics without sustained effort.

Although all the attention was on the senior national team, 2012 also proved to be a big year for Simone. The work paid off. The sacrifices proved worth it.

At the American Classic held at the Ranch, she placed first in vault, third on beam, fourth on bars, and tied for second on floor, winning the all-around title. At the U.S. Classic in Chicago, she won all-around again. Then in June, she returned to the National Championship, this time held in St. Louis, Missouri.

A year prior it had been the worst experience of her career, a loss that caused her to reconsider her future as a gymnast. Now she was prepared and experienced.

Now she was an elite performer.

Simone finished third in all-around, leaving no doubt that she was now a different gymnast.

Best of all, she took first in vault by pushing herself to perform the Amanar. Over the year she had built up her confidence to the point that attempting the move was no longer a cause of panic. She didn't just perform it, either; she performed it almost perfectly, receiving a 9.300 from the judges. That she attempted it at all was nearly enough on its own to earn her a respectable score. Her 6.500 degree of difficulty was tied for the highest in the meet. She was no longer at a disadvantage.

After the event, her life started to change quickly.

Simone received greater attention in the gymnastics world as she positioned herself for the senior national team in 2013, when she would turn sixteen. Expectations were now higher. Every time she thought she had given everything she could, there was Aimee or Martha demanding more.

Simone couldn't hide anymore. All eyes were on

her. Unfortunately, she still continued to occasionally lack focus in practice and at times it showed in meets. At the Secret U.S. Classic that year, she even had to drop out after three events due to a combination of poor concentration and an injury. Simone also wasn't the easiest person to coach.

"She was defiant," Martha said.

"I think it just comes out of my stubbornness, that I don't kind of listen to what people say sometimes if I don't like it," Simone said.

This would be the struggle of her career. Could she accept the coaching? Martha even brought her to the Karolyi Ranch for some individual training. It was a sign of how bright a future USA Gymnastics believed Simone might have.

"I reassured her about her potential, but also reminded her that the talent by itself doesn't make the results," Martha said at the time. "You have to have very diligent and very consistent, disciplined work on a daily basis to be able to build up your confidence level. If you have that confidence, that's the only way you will be able to perform in competitions."

As she approached the National Championships, Simone began to have another breakthrough. She started seeing a sports psychologist, who was there to coach her mentally the way Aimee coached her physically. Both mental toughness and physical toughness are important to succeed in sports.

Simone explained to her psychologist that sometimes she practiced poorly because she was overwhelmed with concern over how others were judging her.

"He said, 'Do you ever do that when you compete?'" Simone said. "I said 'no.' And he said, 'Why were you doing it that day?'

"I kind of stepped back and thought about it, 'Yeah, he's right,'" Simone continued. "And ever since then, I just try to have fun and block out what everybody else says."

Yes, she needed to concentrate and work hard, but she always performed well when the competition was considered fun, not when it was considered work. If she could remain "bubbly" and "bouncy," then perhaps that would help. No longer would she be afraid to smile.

"I think that is what helps me," Simone said. "If you are having fun that is when you are doing your best."

The 2013 National Championships were held in Hartford, Connecticut, that year and Simone was no longer in the junior competition. This was the main event. Both McKayla Maroney and Kyla Ross, heroes of the 2012 Olympics, were competing. Simone had never faced competition like this. Yet, rather than worry, she had fun and trusted her training.

And just like that, no one could stop her. She led after day one and then took the all-around title by finishing second in all four events. She was the best gymnast in America, and a true all-around master. As a testament to her training, it was her strong scores in all the events, not just in vault or floor, that drove her to the championship.

Simone was almost stunned that she won. She declared it "no big deal" after and claimed, "I thought even if I did come in second, third, everybody looked good, so I was happy."

The victory set her up to compete at the 2013 World Championships in Belgium, as part of an exclusive five-person team along with fellow elite gymnasts Kyla Ross, McKayla Maroney, Elizabeth Price, and Brenna Dowell.

"Everybody knows the [Secret] Classic wasn't her best competition, which was just three weeks ago," Martha said, "and in these three weeks, we had great progress on consistency. If we can achieve the same amount of progress in the remaining month before the World Championship, I think we will be in a good place."

How good a place was the question.

# 8
# Worlds

**S**IMONE HAD COMPETED IN A FEW international meets, but nothing like the World Championships.

The competition, the pressure, the stakes at hand, it could all prove overwhelming. Here were the best of the best, not just in the United States but all the historic gymnastic powers around the world, such as Aliya Mustafina of Russia, Yao Jinnan of China, Larisa Iordache of Romania, and Vanessa Ferrari of Italy. Some of them were former World Champions and Olympians with far more experience.

And now Simone was on unfamiliar ground, in

Antwerp, Belgium, where the food is different, the hotels are different, everything is slightly different.

In Simone's new effort to remain calm, she came up with two tricks to keep her grounded in what otherwise was the most stressful and uncertain week of her life. One was simply to not worry about what she didn't know. Fear of the unknown is a powerful emotion. It's also mostly pointless. Why let something that may not even happen impact how you prepare for what you know will?

"She said she had never been to Worlds before so she didn't know what to expect," Aimee said. "She said, 'So I'm not going to be nervous.'"

That helped. So too did her idea of making sure she looked at Martha just before each routine. Martha had a way of grounding her, making it all seem like they were back in Texas at a training session. The rest of the arena, the crowd, and the noise would just fade away.

"I knew if I had her in my line of sight, I wouldn't mess up," Simone wrote in *Courage to Soar*.

Simone was aided by the rotation of events—up first was vault, where she felt comfortable and where nearly two years of pushing herself to attempt more difficult moves could pay off. Kyla Ross was clean on her double-twisting Yurchenko to earn a score of 15.366, but Simone followed that with an Amanar—basically a two-and-a-half-twisting Yurchenko. She took the lead at 15.850. Degree of difficulty paid off.

Kyla would prove to be Simone's chief competition. The California native was tall for a gymnast, nearly a foot taller than Simone. As such, she is considered a more fluid and eloquent gymnast, something that was a big advantage before the scoring system began rewarding the difficulty of routines. That change in scoring evened things out for powerhouse tumblers such as Simone.

Despite being competitors, the two had become great friends—"best friends," Simone said—throughout the process, so while they were fighting for a World Championship, they were also supporting and encouraging each other.

Kyla proved slightly better on the bars—15.100 to 14.700—but Simone still led halfway through. Simone then delivered an excellent beam routine, including a front aerial that led to a split jump and a dismount featuring two back handsprings to a full twist double back. She was pleased with her 14.433. Kyla was just a bit more perfect, scoring a 14.533 and taking a slight lead of 0.16.

Last up, however was floor, which was ideal for Simone. Kyla's routine couldn't match Simone's in terms of difficulty. While Kyla performed her routine almost flawlessly, she mustered only a respectable, but not incredible, 14.333.

Simone knew that if she performed well, she would win. Part of the reason Simone's degree of difficulty was so high was that she was going to attempt a move that was new to gymnastics. For months she and Aimee had been working on a double layout—body fully extended as it rotated through the air—with a twist. It was the twist that was new.

The move had no name at the time, but Simone knew that per gymnastics tradition, if she hit it at the World Championships (or Olympics), it would become known as "the Biles." For a girl who just a year prior hadn't known what her future held, Simone was now one routine away from being crowned the best gymnast on the planet, with her own signature move to go down in history.

Wearing a sparkling pink leotard, Simone tried to put all that out of mind. She took the floor, looked at Martha, and got in position. She crushed her first tumbling run and then lined up for the second— where the double layout with a twist would be performed. She sprinted down the mat and went into a round-off, then a back handspring and then two soaring layouts, her body as straight as an arrow. Just before landing she completed the twist . . . perfectly.

The crowd in Belgium roared with delight! They knew they had witnessed something historic—the creation of a new move and the birth of a new gymnastics star. A minute later, Simone finished with a beaming smile as cheers fell down all around her. She walked to the edge and got a big hug from Aimee.

"On floor, I just have a lot of fun," Simone said. "That is the main key."

Minutes later her score of 15.233 (6.500 difficulty, 8.733 execution, both tops for the competition) flashed on the board. No other competitor had come close to her on floor—the second highest was 14.700, a whopping .533 behind.

Simone was the champion of the world. Kyla would take silver.

"It hasn't sunken in," Simone said after. "I still can't believe it."

Up in the stands her family cheered and cried tears of joy. It had been a long, slow process, but also one that quickly came together at the end. The key was Simone believing in herself, and once that happened the gymnastics took care of itself.

"Lots of psychological work," Martha said.

Simone almost didn't know what to do with herself. She was overwhelmed by the victory and soon she and Kyla were shuffled up to the podium (Aliya Mustafina of Russia won bronze). Standing on top, she watched the American flag rise and listened to "The Star Spangled Banner." She was the first black woman to win the all-around title at the World Championships. It was almost everything she'd ever dreamed of.

"It is exciting to hear the national anthem; it is such an honor to represent the United States," Simone said.

As much as she wanted to celebrate with her family and relax from the stress, the meet wasn't over. After the all-around, the meet turns to individual events, which were spread over two additional days of competition. Due to her strong performances, Simone had qualified for all of them.

Simone took silver on vault, trailing teammate McKayla Maroney. And she just missed out on a medal on bars, coming in 4th by only 0.313 points. The next day, she took bronze on beam and then cruised to gold on floor, giving her two golds and four medals total in her first World Championships.

"Amazing," Simone said.

When she returned to Texas, Simone was a hero—not just at Bannon's but nearly everywhere she went. She made television appearances. Her face was plastered on gymnastics magazines that she used to read to find out more about her heroes. Now, she was one herself. She couldn't have been happier.

Yet there was also a negative side. One morning Simone woke up, checked her social media, and saw there was a major controversy surrounding her. Her accounts were flooded with messages and arguments. Simone was confused until she and her mom figured out what had happened.

An Italian gymnast named Carlotta Ferlito had told a newspaper reporter about a conversation she'd had with her teammate Vanessa Ferrari in which she said, "Next time we should paint our skin black so then we can win, too."

The implication was that Simone had received her high scores and made history only because she was black (just one year after Gabby Douglas became the first black woman to win Olympic gold in the individual all-around).

The comments caused an uproar in the media and the gymnastics world. Simone's parents shot back. They knew how hard their daughter had worked and how much she had sacrificed to be crowned world champion. They weren't going to let anyone suggest Simone hadn't earned it fair and square.

"I found it very insulting," Ron Biles told *USA Today*. "The racial comment was really out of line."

What particularly hurt was that Simone had been raised to see herself as an athlete, a student, a sister, a person that went beyond the color of her skin. She had competed in a sport that was overwhelmingly white without ever making race a big deal. She had a diverse group of friends. She respected competitors from all nationalities and backgrounds.

When people noted that she was the first black woman to win a World Championship, she was proud of that, but mostly downplayed it. Many people wanted to focus on her race, either as a positive (a sense of pride for the African American community) or because her victories threatened the long-established power in the sport (mostly Europeans winning medals).

Simone wanted to avoid that. Whatever obstacles she'd overcome to get to this level were left quiet.

She just wanted to be known as Simone Biles. Yet now she was being criticized anyway, with people saying she was gaining an advantage due to the color of her skin.

"Normally it's not in her favor being black, at least not in the world that I live in," Ron Biles said, citing the racism that has disadvantaged black people in sports and the rest of society for centuries.

Simone said she actually wasn't even that offended by what Carlotta Ferlito said. "I figured she was just disappointed in the outcome of the meet," Simone wrote in *Courage to Soar*. "When you're not in a good place, you can say the wrong thing."

Indeed, soon after, Ferlito took to Twitter to apologize.

"I've made a mistake, I'm not perfect," Ferlito wrote. "I was too nervous and I didn't think about what I was saying. I'm just a human. I'm so sorry . . . I didn't want to be rude or racist. I love Simone."

That was enough for Simone, but unfortunately the controversy didn't die down. In a statement, the Italian Gymnastics Federation tried to explain things and made it all even worse.

"The sport is about maximizing what natural talent a person has in gymnastics at this moment, which is going towards a technique that opens up new chances to athletes of color (well-known for power) while penalizing the more artistic Eastern European style that allowed Russians and Romanians to dominate the sport for years."

This was the same old argument coming up—pointing out how the new scoring system favored degree of difficulty, which requires athleticism, rather than what a judge might consider artistic. It was ridiculous, however. It was nothing more than a continuation of the racist assumption that has existed in sports for ages, the false idea that black athletes specialize in raw physical power over grace and technical knowledge/ability. An idea that has been proven wrong and offensive time and again. Besides, people of all races come in all different body types.

Indeed, Simone was short and powerful. So was Olympic champion Shawn Johnson, who was white and stood four foot eleven. She was known for her tumbling more than the elegance that a taller competitor, such as Kyla Ross, might be able to utilize. The sport is about each individual doing their best—no matter their size or body type. Thinking otherwise is simply ignorant.

"Why aren't there blacks in swimming?" an Italian gymnastics spokesperson wrote on Facebook. "Because the sport doesn't suit their physical characteristics. Is gymnastics becoming the same thing, to the point of wanting to be colored?"

That remark led to even more outrage, particularly because there's a clear history in the US of black people being discouraged from swimming and limiting their access to the sport. On top of that, at the 2012 Olympics, an African American swimmer named Cullen Jones won gold for the United States, and at the 2016 Games, Simone Manuel would win two golds and two silvers. The racist past related to black people and swimming made these wins all the more historic and groundbreaking.

The Italian president eventually apologized, but the damage was done. Simone decided to not let it bother her. She declined to say anything about it to the media.

"I wanted every child, regardless of race, to be able . . . to know that following your dreams—not just in gymnastics, but in everything—shouldn't have anything to do with the color of your skin," Simone wrote in *Courage to Soar*. "It should only be about finding the discipline and the courage to do the hard work."

Simone knew she had won because of her work and her talent, not because of the color of her skin. If someone else couldn't handle that, then it was their problem, not hers.

Besides, they had better get used to it, because it wasn't like she was going anywhere.

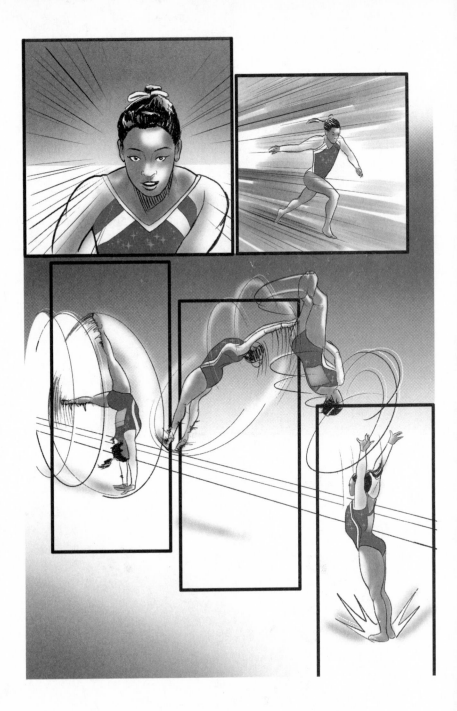

# 9

# Dominance

**F**RESHLY MINTED as a world champion, Simone made it clear that one very important goal of hers remained unfulfilled—earning a spot at the Olympics. The problem? The next one wasn't until 2016, nearly three years away. Staying motivated and sharp until then was not going to be easy.

Especially since 2014 proved to be a year of transitions and uncertainty for Simone. Most notably, she injured her shoulder training at the Ranch and needed to sit out of competition for six months. Doctors said she'd be fine in the long run, but not being able to train at her normal level made Simone uncomfortable.

Another big change came when Aimee decided to leave Bannon's Gymnastix, where she'd worked for two decades. None of it had to do with Simone, it was just time for a change. Simone and her parents, however, were loyal to Aimee, not the gym, so they said they'd go wherever Aimee wound up.

When there wasn't an obvious option, Simone's parents decided to solve the problem themselves. Simone's mother was involved in a business that owned some nursing homes. She decided that she would sell the nursing homes and use the money to build their own gym—a modern, massive, 52,000-square-foot facility called the World Champions Centre (WCC) in Spring, Texas, outside Houston.

The Biles family may not have known anything about gymnastics when Simone and Adria first signed up, but at this point they knew just about everything, including how lucrative of a business it could be.

They figured if they built a top-end facility and used Simone's name recognition, they could create a very successful business and be the top gymnasium in the Houston area. The building would have room for other activities, too—dance, cheerleading, trampoline, ninja warrior, tae kwon do, parties, and so on. There'd be a fitness center, a merchandise store, a café, and comfortable places for parents to wait and work while their kids were training. There'd even be a classroom where elite athletes could take a homeschool curriculum.

It would be perfect. Aimee would coach Simone and some other top students there. The only downside is you can't put a building like that up overnight. It wouldn't be ready until 2015. In the meantime, Aimee set up shop at another gym for six months and then spent one year in a converted warehouse. It wasn't much to look at it—inside or out—and it certainly wasn't the kind of place that a world champion usually trains at, but it would do. The equipment was the equipment. And Aimee was still Simone's coach.

Even with the injury, Simone didn't skip a beat.

After resting for a few months, she won the all-around National Championship in Pittsburgh in dominating fashion, beating Kyla Ross 122.55 to 118.30. The difficulty of her bar routine had been downgraded until her shoulder was fully recovered, but it hardly mattered. Neither did the fact that she fell during the beam final.

No one could compete with Simone. No one was even close to her. Simone also took individual golds in vault and floor, and silver in beam.

Almost as notable was Simone's smile throughout the week. This was her second National Championship and she was no longer a nervous newcomer. She was the veteran defending champion, and so she further embraced her theory that the happier she was the better she performed.

That meant playing to the crowd, especially during her floor routine or between events. She was known to wink at fans. "That's what they pay for," Simone said of the fans. "That's what they came to see."

There were lots of smiles and laughs as Simone had the time of her life out there, loose and free. She even became known for relentlessly encouraging and congratulating other competitors, despite the fact that they were out to defeat her.

"We're all going through the exact same thing," Simone said. "We're kind of like family. I just think of them as friends, and we always need that little lift, so we give it to each other."

Sometimes, at international meets, Martha had to remind her to stop cheering on opponents that were trying to beat Team USA. Simone had to learn to stop herself when a gold was on the line.

"She has this amazing smile and way about her throughout the competition that shows she truly enjoys the sport," said Shannon Miller, the first American to win consecutive all-around World Championships in 1993 and 1994. "At the same time, her skill level and ease during routines can't help but completely intimidate the other competitors."

"She just projects herself," Aimee said at Nationals. "She's a happy person. We talk about making her gymnastics joyful. The more she cheers for people, the more relaxed she is."

There was plenty to cheer about at the World Championship that fall in Nanning, China. Team USA rolled to the team gold with a score of 179.280, easily outpacing China (172.587) and Russia (171.462).

Then Simone became the first American since Shannon Miller two decades prior to repeat as all-around world champion. She beat Romania's Larisa Iordache 60.231 to 59.765. Kyla got the bronze.

In case that wasn't enough, Simone added individual golds in beam and floor, and a silver on vault. Her performance was so strong that fans, media, and others had begun to run out of adjectives to describe her. No one had ever seen someone who was so much stronger than the competition.

"Simone is Simone," said Shannon Miller. "There is no one else like her. Her power and strength are absolutely stunning. She makes the most difficult skills look like a walk in the park . . . Barring injury, I can't see anyone coming close to Simone Biles."

"She's not human," gymnastics legend Mary Lou Retton said. "She may be the most talented I've ever seen in my life, honestly. And I don't think she's tapped into what she can really do. I think she's unbeatable."

Truthfully, everyone is beatable on a given day, although Simone had now not lost an individual meet since she withdrew from the U.S. Secret Classic in July 2013.

That streak continued through 2015, where Simone remained undefeated. She won the American Classic by the largest margin in history—4.467 points over MyKayla Skinner—by coming in first in all four events. "I was most pleased with bars," Simone noted. She then won the all-around title at the National Championship (her third in a row) while adding individual first in vault and beam, plus a silver on floor.

Simone said her ability to consistently reach new heights came not in trying to be better than the other gymnasts, but in trying to be better than she had ever been before. That, she said, was the only thing she could control. Not what other competitors were doing or how fans compared her to past gymnastics greats.

"It's truly [a matter of wanting] to be the best version of me and I don't want to replicate others," Simone said. "Because a lot of people compare to other people a bunch, but I just want to go out there and I just want to be Simone."

She then traveled to Scotland, where she led the US to team gold (again) and won golds in the all-around (again), beam (again), and floor (again). That gave her a record ten gold medals at World Championships. On vault she took bronze.

Simone by this point had built her routines up so high that their degree of difficulty made her nearly impossible to beat. Gabby Douglas finished second at that meet, and her combined degrees of difficulty were 24.300. Simone's came to 25.500, including a whopping 6.800 on floor. It meant Simone could stumble and still beat a perfect Douglas, or anyone else.

Indeed, Simone stepped out of bounds on her second tumbling run on floor and still won easily.

"On floor, I'd never gone out of bounds before, but I guess there's a first for everything," Simone said.

Regardless of that misstep, she had once again crushed the competition. Fittingly, she said she had a saying on her phone that read: "Blow Your Own Mind."

"I think that's what I did." She smiled.

The medals were, of course, great, but in some ways, they weren't even the goal. Aimee and Simone knew how good she was and so they pointed to just doing the routines well and then letting the results happen. They didn't enter meets anymore saying, "we need to win gold" or "we need to medal." There was just one objective: Perform to the best of your ability.

"We don't talk about placement at meets or what our goal is to place at a meet," Aimee said.

About the only thing that happened during this period that Simone couldn't control came during the 2014 World Championships. She was standing atop the medal podium, just after the playing of the national anthem, when she noticed that there was a bee in the bouquet of flowers she had been given. Simone, so fearless when hurling her body blindly through the air, shrieked in terror, jumped off the podium, and threw the flowers down.

The bee eventually flew into Kyla Ross's flowers, but she just calmly placed them down and then went to pose for pictures. Kyla was as cool and calm as ever.

The video of Simone being "attacked" by the bee went viral, another humorous moment in her life. It was also one that showed that no matter how fierce or commanding Simone was in competition, she was still mostly a silly, excitable seventeen-year-old outside it. Maybe this wasn't the traditional personality of a great gymnast, but Simone didn't care.

She was the best in the world and there was nothing anyone could do about that.

# 10

# The Olympics

**A**FTER THREE CONSECUTIVE World Championships, Simone had a decision to make. She was headed into 2016, at last an Olympic year, and she had positioned herself as a likely breakout star of the upcoming Games. If she did in Rio de Janeiro, Brazil, what she had been doing for the last three years, she was going to become a household name—even for non–gymnastics fans.

That's the power of the Olympics. Every four years, people who otherwise don't know the difference between a cartwheel and a round-off tune in to the Games and watch gymnastics. The best American, sometimes even a couple of them, can generate incredible media attention and thus have the ability to make a lot of money promoting products, starring in commercials, and selling books and documentaries, or giving speeches.

There was a long list of companies that wanted to sign Simone to an endorsement deal so they could capitalize on the run-up to, and mostly the excitement after, the Olympics. To sign those deals, Simone would have to turn professional and hire a sports agent, a marketing company, a financial planner, and so on. Lots of grown-up stuff.

Until then she'd focused almost solely on her training. Her parents had taken care of everything else. Becoming a pro would move her into adulthood. It would also mean she'd have to give up on her longtime dream of competing in college gymnastics.

By this time, Simone had committed to accept a full scholarship to UCLA, a gymnastics powerhouse that is located in Los Angeles, California. She thought it would be another fun experience in her life and career. However, the National Collegiate Athletic Association (NCAA), which oversees college sports, doesn't allow professional athletes, or anyone who has an endorsement contract, to compete. College sports is supposed to be amateur.

Simone had a decision to make.

Really, though, it wasn't much of a choice. Simone could make millions of dollars by turning pro. And she could still attend UCLA as a student—and more than pay for the tuition. She just couldn't compete for the gymnastics team. It was a good compromise.

With that, Simone quickly signed endorsement deals with Nike, Hershey's Chocolate, Kellogg's, and Procter & Gamble, which produces lots of household brands such as Tide laundry detergent, Ivory soap, and Bounty paper towels. The deals were worth a reported $4 million. Simone was suddenly a very wealthy eighteen-year-old. And she enrolled as a student at UCLA.

But before stepping foot on UCLA's campus, Simone had other business to attend to.

On Tuesday, July 26, 2016, Simone and her US teammates boarded a plane in Houston and flew to Rio de Janeiro, Brazil, for the Olympics. They had just completed a grueling ten-day training session at the Karolyi Ranch that would serve as a final tune-up. They were equal parts exhausted and excited.

For Simone, this was her dream come true. Growing up, she had wanted nothing more than the chance to compete in the Olympics. At that time, she didn't set her sights on winning gold or any medal, just on competing on the ultimate stage. The destination was enough. Of course, she wasn't going to the Olympics just to go to the Olympics. She was going to win. So were her teammates.

The five-gymnast team included 2016 Olympics stars Gabby Douglas and Aly Raisman, plus fellow first-time Olympians Laurie Hernandez and Madison Kocian. Aly, who at twenty-two was the oldest member of the team and was dubbed "Mama Aly" by the others due to her motherly ways, told them there was nothing to be nervous about. The Olympics might feel like a big deal, but it was just like World Championships, only with lots of banners bearing the Olympic rings.

Simone wasn't so sure. She was clearly the best gymnast in the world, and she had performed the routines, leaps, and dismounts that she would break out in Rio hundreds of times so they would feel like an old habit, but she was still a bit terrified. This was, no matter what Aly said, the Olympics, after all.

It really hit home when, after landing in Rio, their

bus pulled up to the Olympic Village, a collection of white high-rises built just down the street from where many of the competitions, including gymnastics, would be staged.

Team USA had its own building, and Simone and her teammates shared a four-bedroom suite on the third floor. Simone and Laurie took one room and Aly and Madison another. Gabby had her own room, as did a trainer with the team. There were shared bathrooms, plus a living room and a balcony.

Downstairs there were common areas for athletes to hang out, a cafeteria with just about every food in the world available twenty-four hours a day, a swimming pool, jogging trails, and other luxuries. It was incredible.

Sometimes they'd get starstruck and try to get selfies with other famous athletes such as Jamaican sprinter Usain Bolt. Other times they'd get recognized and have other Olympians approach them for photos. Then there were all the hours they just sat on the balcony and hardly believed they had made it.

"It's been an incredible journey," Simone said at the time. "It's very exciting. Every day we wake up we are like, 'Wow, we are here, we are at the Olympics.'"

There were only a couple of downsides. One was

that she and her teammates were completely isolated from their families. In an effort to avoid distractions, Martha would only permit one or two visits during the entire Olympics. So while Simone's parents, sister, and brothers came to Brazil, she couldn't see them.

The other was that they had to skip the famed Opening Ceremonies, where the torch is lit and a parade of athletes from each country walks into a massive stadium. Everyone around the world who has ever watched the Olympics has wanted to be a part of that. However, doing so requires athletes to line up and stand for up to five hours, a physical toll that Simone and the others couldn't risk. Also, due to the huge crowds, it's not uncommon for athletes to make it back to the Olympic Village at two or three a.m. It works for certain athletes or ones that compete later in the Games, but since the ceremony was on a Friday night and gymnastics qualification began on Sunday, it was too close for Simone and the others.

"We have to watch on television from the Village," Simone said.

The extra rest certainly paid off at Sunday's qualifying, which would determine who was eligible to compete in the finals of each event, as Simone and Team USA were absolutely brilliant.

As a team, they earned a total of 185.238 points, nearly a full ten ahead of China (175.279) and Russia (174.620). That established the Americans as the overwhelming favorite to win team gold, which was their number one goal.

That was just the beginning for the members of Team USA. Simone and Aly qualified for all-around. Gabby would have also since her scores were high enough, except the Olympics limits finalists to just two per country.

Simone also qualified for the individual vault, beam, and floor competitions. She actually had the highest qualifying score in each of those events, plus the all-around. That meant Simone had a legitimate chance to win five gold medals, which would be an Olympic record (four had last been done by Vera Caslavska of then Czechoslovakia in 1968).

Meanwhile, Madison and Gabby qualified on bars, Laurie on beam, and Aly on floor. Each of the Americans would not just be seeking team gold together, but pushing for individual medals as well.

"It felt incredible," Simone said. "Every one of us qualified for an event final so I don't think we could ask for anything more and we have something to look forward to. I think that is very special for all of us because we cheer each other on."

Simone was all about the team mentality. Gymnastics is an individual sport, and she'd experienced years and years of solo workouts in Bannon's and the WCC. Despite that isolation, or perhaps because of it, Simone was most excited about the chance to succeed *alongside* her teammates and cheer them on, just like they cheered her on every step of the way.

And while the USA team members were technically competing against one another in individual competitions, the other four Americans knew firsthand that Simone was the best one there. They were just glad she was on their side.

"We are all family," Aly said.

The family was focused on winning team gold. The Americans had won team gold in 1996 and 2012, and this was a chance to win consecutive Olympics for the first time ever. Gabby and Aly were particularly interested in defending their title. Everyone knew that the US was the favorite, but everyone also knew they had to deliver on this grandest of stages.

One key element was the need to build a tight team bond. Training together had helped. Living together in the Olympic Village even more so. They all liked to hang out together and even prepare for the meet together. It was a sisterhood.

"I think it is always very exciting to put on our leos and do our hair and makeup together," Simone said. "It is just something we like to do. I think together we are so strong and it motivates each and every one of us."

Still, heading into the competition, there were butterflies.

It was only natural. Aimee had noticed a hint of nerves among the team. She knew the stakes were so high and the crowd so big and noisy inside the 12,000-seat Rio Olympic Arena that the team was slightly rattled.

"They were a little more tense in the warm-up area, so I reminded them to do what they've been doing in practice and really feed off the energy of the crowd and do it from a place of joy," Aimee said. "I wanted the energy in the arena to boost them up as opposed to make them tense up."

The first rotation was vault, and the Americans jumped to an early lead with Laurie, Aly, and Simone, who, in her first Olympic performance that mattered, was incredible. Her Amanar didn't just have her tied for the highest degree of difficulty on vault (6.300), her execution score of 9.633 was the highest handed out in that event. The US led by 0.700 off the bat.

Simone, Gabby, and Madison then crushed it on bars to extend the lead to 4.026 after the second rotation. It was Gabby (15.766) and Madison (15.933) who led—Simone's score was "just" 14.800, but Simone loved that. This was about the team. The Simone Show could wait. If anything, this made it easier for her.

"I don't think you feel pressure whenever your teammates go up and hit," Simone said. "You almost feel confident that you can go do it too because once the first person goes it sort of sets a rhythm. That makes us so excited once we see our teammates hit. You're up there and you're like, 'I've got this, it's just one more routine.' That gets us hyped."

On beam, Aly, Laurie, and then Simone continued the momentum (scoring a team beam high of 15.300), and the US led by an overwhelming 4.961 after three events. Everyone was sticking their routines. Everyone was performing with confidence. Everyone was smiling and hugging and having fun.

All those hours of work. All those grueling sessions at the Karolyi Ranch. All the times they executed the routines, over and over, no matter how tired or stressed, were proving beneficial.

With a huge lead going into floor, there was no longer a reason to be nervous. Laurie reminded Aly and Simone that they just needed to get through their routines and they'd win gold. This was the time to have fun.

And Simone, in particular, loves to have fun.

She had created a special routine for the Olympics. It was incredibly challenging. The combination of an opening "Biles"—double layout with a twist—as well as a tucked double-double late gave her a meet-high 6.700 degree of difficulty.

She also had USA Gymnastics choreographer Dominic Zito come up with a Brazilian-themed dance—full of salsa moves—that played perfectly with a five-song mix that included excerpts from the soundtrack of the animated movie *Rio* as well as another song called "Brazil." She wanted to honor, and hopefully engage with, the local fans.

"Dominic made up that routine for me and he put the music in for me," Simone said. "Martha liked it and I liked it."

And the fans loved it. They clapped along to the songs, screamed at how high she tumbled, and eventually thundered down applause at the end as

Simone anchored the incredible Team USA performance. Simone was having the time of her life.

When she finished, her teammates mobbed her. They knew they had won gold. The scores confirmed the obvious—an event-high 9.100 in execution for a 15.800 total. The Americans had defeated the silver medalist Russians by a whopping 8.209 points.

"I was just excited about how calm I kept it, just like in practice," Simone said. "I didn't let the stress or the nerves or even being the last one up and no one else and the crowd just looking at me get to me. So I was very excited whenever I landed my dismount. I was just like, 'Oh my gosh, we are done.'"

Soon all five of them were up on the podium together, gold medals hanging from their necks, hands over their hearts, listening to "The Star Spangled Banner" play and watching the American flag rise up. It felt, to Simone, like the greatest night of her life, the culmination of a forever dream.

No matter what was to come in individual events, she was an Olympic gold medalist and she had done it with a bunch of her closest friends.

"It doesn't even seem real," Simone said. "When we wake up, we're going to see it and then believe it."

# 11

# Superstar

**F**IRST, SIMONE WAS an instrumental part of the team gold victory. Then she won gold in the all-around. Up next, three individual events she had qualified for—vault, beam, floor. Three more competitions on three consecutive days. This would be the ultimate challenge, a mental grind of trying to remain sharp each and every day with no break in sight.

Since she had qualified first in all three events, the media and fans were talking about Simone winning each of them. That would give her a record five gold medals in a single Olympics. It was dubbed "The Drive for Five."

For Simone, winning all three seemed too grand to consider. Aimee was concerned that the quest might prove overwhelming. She kept telling Simone the same thing: "Other people's expectations are not your expectations."

Simone leaned back on her training. In gymnastics, you can only concentrate on what you are currently doing. Thinking about anything else, let alone a routine that was days away, was foolish. If you slip up on the task in front of you, you can get injured, let alone fail. Even the simplest of moves can do you in.

So when the media asked her about winning three more golds, she just shrugged. Maybe it would happen. Maybe it wouldn't. Besides, the only way she could possibly pull it off was by ignoring all the noise.

"I just have to stay focused," Simone said.

That wasn't easy. After her incredible performances in team and in all-around, Simone was now a full-blown celebrity. The media couldn't get enough of her. She was constantly surrounded by a crowd of reporters looking for any chance they could to talk to her. At the Olympic Village, other athletes stopped her for selfies. Her social media accounts blew up with well wishes.

Simone and Laurie would sit in their room, scrolling through their phones in disbelief at all the celebrities who were suddenly fans . . . of theirs.

Kim Kardashian West. Samuel L. Jackson. Hillary Clinton. Leslie Jones. Tori Kelly. J.J. Watt. Gabrielle Union. Even President Barack and Michelle Obama extended well wishes.

"Me and Laurie will scream in the room every time something happens," Simone said, laughing at herself. "And it's like, 'What happened, happened?' We think we are pretty normal."

Amid the media frenzy, Simone and the team went on the *Today Show*, where she revealed that her celebrity crush was Zac Efron. They exchanged tweets. Then a few days later, the gymnasts were back on the *Today Show* . . . and there was a surprise waiting for Simone.

"If you bring him out, I am going to pass out," Simone shouted.

Sure enough, they brought out Zac Efron. He had flown all the way from America to Rio de Janeiro, just to visit with the gymnasts. Simone was so nervous, she ran and hid behind Aly. Finally they hugged and snapped selfies.

"When I found out Simone and this team were fans, I was like, 'What kind of guy am I if I don't show up,'" Zac said on *Today*.

This was the kind of whirlwind Simone was suddenly living in. It was like a dream come true. Yet she had to continue to compete.

First up, vault. And her first vault was the ever-difficult Amanar, which requires two and a half twists in the backward salto position. Simone had no problem in the air. When she landed, however, she took a small hop to find her balance. She frowned.

"She wasn't exactly happy with her first vault," Aimee said. "She thought she could have done better."

This was the mind-set Simone had learned from Martha. Worry about your performance, not about the judges. In this case, what Simone thought wasn't good enough, the judges liked very much. They gave her an execution score of 9.600 (higher than any other gymnast), which, tacked on to her difficulty score of 6.300, put her in first place.

It was the latest example of Simone simply competing at another level. How can someone be in first place at the Olympics and wish they had done better?

For her second and final vault, Simone had upgraded her routine with the Cheng in an effort to assure victory. The Cheng called for her to round-off onto the board, do a half turn onto the vault, then push into a layout front flip with one and a half twists. It carried a 6.400 degree of difficulty.

"I'd been working on the Cheng for on and off like a year," Simone said.

Simone stuck it with near perfection, earning a 9.633 execution score for a total of 16.033. With an average score of 15.966, she easily won gold by 0.715.

So obvious was her victory that other competitors congratulated her even before her final score came in. When it was announced, Biles hardly reacted. She now had three gold medals. It was becoming old hat. She was asked if she even realized that she was dominating these Olympics.

"Sometimes I lay in bed and I'm impressed with myself," she said. "[I say,] 'Simone, you did it.' [Then I say,] 'Yes, I did.'"

Up next: beam. This, Simone knew, would be the toughest of the individual finals. The last one would be floor, where she was an overwhelming favorite. On beam, however, anything can happen. Anyone can fall.

In this case, Simone didn't fall, but she did slip and almost fall. It actually took an impressive save just to stay on the beam and finish her routine. She wasn't happy when it ended.

"I'm not going to medal with that routine," she told Aimee.

Aimee wasn't so sure. No, it wasn't peak Simone. Gold seemed out of reach. But Simone's score of 14.733 was still very good, and after the other gymnasts cycled through, it proved enough to win bronze. Dutch gymnast Sanne Wevers won gold with a 15.466 while Laurie Hernandez took silver with a 15.333, much to the delight of her teammates.

Simone was so surprised she had medaled at all, she wasn't ready for the ceremony.

"Yes, she is human," Aimee said. "But I don't know how she made that save because both her feet were coming off the beam. So I was pretty impressed with that. That took superhuman power."

The Drive for Five was over. Simone didn't mind. Yes, she wanted to win, but mainly she just wanted to perform better.

"It was still a good beam routine," Simone said. "I'm still pretty proud of it."

Simone wasn't going to complain about a bronze medal.

"She won the bronze medal on beam at the Olympics," Aimee said. "How many people get to do that?"

Simone admitted that the long Olympics and all the pressure-filled routines had worn her down a bit. Did she still have any energy left? she was asked.

"I have enough to do a floor routine," Simone said, smiling.

Of course she did. The next day she returned once more. She had been in Rio for over three weeks, working out nearly every single day. There had been one day of qualifications and now five days of medal competition. It was tiring, but floor was her favorite. She could tumble. She could fly. She could dance. She could interact with the Brazilian crowds that had come to love watching her perform.

"I think floor is the perfect way to end it," she said.

In some ways, the pressure was off. No more expectations about winning five golds, although Simone had mostly brushed that off anyway.

"I think the pressure I put on myself is more than I [take] in from the media or anyone else," Simone said. "I just pressure myself to hit my sets."

To say Simone hit all her sets was an understatement. She was nearly perfect. Every landing. Every twist. Every move.

Simone had performed her floor routine three times already at these Olympics. In the qualifications she scored a 15.733. In the team final, a 15.800. In the all-around final, a 15.933. Now in the floor final, she did even better, scoring an astounding 15.966 to easily defeat Aly, who took the silver medal with a 15.500.

Just when fans wondered how Simone could do better, she had soared to new heights and won her fourth gold medal.

"The cherry on top," Simone said.

The floor final was the last day of competition at the Olympics, and thus the last competition for Martha and Bela Karolyi, who were retiring. They had spent decades training the best gymnasts in the world and had become famous in 1976 when Nadia Comăneci became a star. Now, all these years later, they had trained another perfect gymnast.

"Nadia was so much better than anyone else at

her time and Simone is ahead of anyone in the field now," Martha said.

These were two very different gymnasts who competed in very different eras of gymnastics. Back in 1976, execution was everything, whereas these days, the sport is based equally upon the difficulty of the routine. To Martha, though, there were obvious similarities between the two greatest gymnasts of all time.

"Extraordinary mental toughness and an extraordinary confidence level," Martha said. "Each [trait] makes them [less] afraid in this big arena in front of all those judges and all the competitors. They come in and say, 'I have this under my belt, I have worked for this and I can do it.'"

Everywhere Bela Karolyi went in Rio, he kept getting stopped and asked if Simone was the greatest of all time. He had trained Nadia. He had trained Mary Lou Retton. He had been around all the best. He tried to do his best to answer the question about a sport in which the athletes are constantly inventing new and more difficult moves.

"People are asking, 'How did Nadia relate to this? How did Mary Lou relate to this?'" Bela said. "I have to say, those athletes were the greatest of their time. You can't compare because gymnastics is an ongoing thing, constantly changing and more and more complex and difficult sport. So you can't compare Simone Biles played in 2016 vs. Nadia in Montreal in 1976.

"Many times I wonder how far [can] we go?" Bela continued. "[After] Nadia's performance in Montreal, I said, 'Well, maybe this is it. Maybe it changes a little bit [but you can't do better].' Five years later, little kids are playing with the same skills.

"Mary Lou came here with the muscle for tumbling," Bela said. "I said, 'This is it. No one can go higher than this. More power cannot be showcased on the floor.' Five years later, everybody [is doing it]. Now here's Simone, the ultimate, ultimate athlete. Her height [on her jumps] is more superior to anyone I have seen in my life. The closest is Mary Lou with the strength, and explosiveness, and the ultimate temperament to go high. But not this high."

Bela would only declare Simone "one of the greatest in the sport of gymnastics." But there was a reason for that.

He didn't think the world had seen the best Simone Biles they would see. Even with four gold medals and one bronze, the Rio Olympics were not, in his mind, the culmination of Simone's career. There was more potential there. She was just nineteen, injury free, and still deeply motivated. There were more World Championships to come. The 2020 Olympics also.

"She has to stay in the sport," Bela said.

Why?

"I want to see what she does next."

# 12

# Legend

**W**HAT SIMONE DID NEXT was take a break. Her stated post-Olympics goal: "Have fun, live life for a little bit, and see what happens."

What happened was, well, just about everything. After being in the gym almost full-time since the age of six, Simone decided to take off for the rest of 2016 and the entirety of 2017. That gave her body time to heal and allowed her to focus on school, her social life, pretty much anything she wanted. She was now nineteen years old and making a lot of money. It was time to enjoy all that hard work.

And enjoy she did. She visited President and Michelle Obama in the White House. She wrote her autobiography, *Courage to Soar*. She filmed commercials and appeared in magazine shoots. She made a guest appearance as a cheerleader for the Houston Texans of the National Football League. She attended awards shows and met celebrities, who were as eager to get a selfie with her as she was with them.

Mostly, though, she enjoyed time with her friends and family. For years her training schedule had left her with just one day off a week—Sundays. She used to cherish the freedom. Now every day felt like a Sunday. Her biggest challenge was reminding her friends that she hadn't changed.

"I'm still just Simone," she'd tell them. "It's just I have Olympic medals now."

Perhaps the greatest highlight was being a contestant on Season 24 of *Dancing with the Stars*. Simone had been a longtime fan of the show and had cheered on Laurie Hernandez when she won Season 23.

Simone was paired with professional dancer Sasha Farber and the two were considered the favorites to win. This was despite Simone noting, "I can't dance." Fans and judges disagreed, and most weeks

Simone and Sasha ranked near the top of the leaderboard. They were number one after doing the tango in the first week.

They reached the semifinals, but despite receiving perfect scores from the judges in both of their dances, Simone and Sasha were eliminated by fan vote. It was considered a shocking decision, but Simone just smiled. She had long ago taken on the belief that you perform for yourself, and whatever the judges (or in this case viewers) thought didn't matter. Simone might not have been all that experienced with losing (at least of late), but she took it in stride.

"It's okay," Simone said. "I'm just thankful to be at this competition. I think I learned a lot and have matured."

In the summer of 2017, after about a year off, Simone returned to her parents' gym to begin training again. "[The break] was a chance for mind and body to recover," she said.

There was one big difference: Aimee was no longer her coach. Aimee had taken a job coaching and teaching in Florida, and after all those years together, it was believed a fresh start might be good for Simone. They split on good terms and remain friends.

Simone's new coaches were Cecile and Laurent Landi, a husband-and-wife team who hailed from France but had been coaching in Texas for many years. At the 2016 Olympics they had coached Madison Kocian, so Simone was very familiar with not just their coaching style, but also their personalities.

Reenergized after her long break, Simone's goal wasn't just to return to the form that had won her four gold medals and made her the most dominant gymnast on the planet. She wanted to go even further. She was still healthy and now rested and ready to push herself in 2018, 2019, and hopefully in 2020, when the Olympics returned in Tokyo, Japan.

That meant getting back to a six-days-a-week grind in the gym, with long hours, lots of repetition, and, Simone was determined, plenty of laughs and smiles.

But there was a painful side to Simone's return to the gym. Despite the joy she'd experienced in her time off, she'd also endured great hardship. In September 2016, a story in the *Indianapolis Star* newspaper accused former USA Gymnastics national team doctor Larry Nassar of sexually assaulting some of the gymnasts who came to him for treatment. In the coming months, Nassar was arrested and later pleaded guilty to the crimes.

In January 2018, over one hundred gymnasts and former patients testified at his sentencing hearing in Lansing, Michigan, about the abuse they had suffered from a man they trusted and thought was giving them medical treatment. Among those who testified were Aly Raisman and other Olympians.

Simone did not go to court to confront Nassar, but she did release a statement on social media indicating that she had, indeed, been abused by Nassar. Nearly every elite American gymnast over the past couple of decades had been. The scandal rocked both USA Gymnastics specifically and the sport as a whole. It was revealed that Nassar had had the freedom to treat athletes without any supervision, including during international competitions, the Olympics, and even at the Karolyi Ranch.

Simone, like many others, went to therapy in an effort to process being a victim. She and her fellow gymnasts described themselves as survivors. And while they often held great anger at Nassar, they were also angry with USA Gymnastics. The USAG hadn't done enough to protect the young girls entrusted to their care, who were in a very competitive situation and unable to speak up.

"It's not easy coming back to the sport, coming

back to the organization that has failed you," Simone said in 2019. "I feel like every day is a reminder of what I went through and what I've been through and what I'm going through and how I've come out of it.

"We had one job [winning]. And we have done everything that [USA Gymnastics] asked us for—even when we didn't want to. And they couldn't do one job! You had one job, you literally had one job, and you couldn't protect us!"

Almost everyone associated with USA Gymnastics was fired or retired. Some were prosecuted for not doing enough to monitor Nassar, who was sent to prison for the rest of his life. While Martha and Bela Karolyi were not seen as guilty and expressed anger at what Nassar had done, the national training camps moved from the Ranch to the gym in Florida where Aimee now worked. The Karolyis remained in retirement.

It was a sad and difficult time for everyone. Yet Simone was determined to not let being an abuse survivor define or limit her.

She was still the best gymnast in the world and was ready to show it.

At the 2018 National Championships in Boston, Massachusetts, she showed she hadn't lost a step.

She didn't just win her fifth national title in all-around, she also scored the highest in each event over the course of two days. She nabbed the all-around by a huge margin, 6.55 points, over Morgan Hurd, who in 2017, when Simone was on break, had won all-around at the World Championships. Simone was the first gymnast to score highest in every event at Nationals since 1994.

"I didn't think coming into the events this year that I would do as well as I did," Biles said. "I knew I was capable of it, but I kept telling my family, 'I don't know if I'm going to be able to calm myself down the way I did before and handle the nerves.' But so far, so good."

It was beyond good. She left every other gymnast, coach, and fan there stunned by her ability. Even after the long hiatus, there was Simone and there was everyone else.

"She's just in another league, almost," said Riley McCusker, who came in third in all-around. "I'm honestly just in awe of her."

There was more to come. At the 2018 World Championships, Simone again sent a signal that she hadn't slipped and was back to rule the sport. She led the United States to an easy gold in the team competition, blew everyone away for all-around gold, and added four medals in the individual events—gold in vault and floor, silver on bars, and bronze on beam. She was the first gymnast to earn medals in all four events since 1987.

Other than winning gold in all four events, she couldn't have done better. Yet Simone's victories had become so commonplace that when she wobbled on beam and "only" won bronze, fans criticized her on social media. Simone couldn't believe it. She clapped back at them.

"Just saying, I get to decide when I have a disappointing performance," she wrote. "Not y'all over a year out of the sport. Barely a year back in and my first big competition. I'm proud of myself!"

When the competition was over, she explained herself and the unique situation she was in. She was the best in the world, the best of all time, even, and yet some people were still looking for ways to tear her down.

"It's upsetting to me whenever I see all the tweets after the performances of how disappointed they are in me because it's not fair," she said. "They can't set expectations on me. I have to set them on myself."

It made her realize an important lesson. She was

no longer a kid trying to make it. She was no longer dependent on her parents or her coaches or anyone else. She was a grown-up and she needed to continue to compete for herself, not for anyone else. Her fans were great and she loved them. But she wasn't going to worry about what anyone else wanted.

"I feel like this time around I'm doing it for different reasons," Simone said at the 2019 National Championships in Kansas City, Missouri. "The first time around, you do it for yourself but you have a lot of people to prove [things to]. This time, I'm just doing it for myself, and I think that is the beauty of it."

With more to prove to herself—but no one else—she busted out a new move at the 2019 National Championships. She won, of course. She took gold in all-around, vault, beam, and floor. She was third on uneven bars. It was another record, a sixth National Championship.

Yet what caught everyone's attention was a tumbling run she delivered during her floor routine. What was already a challenging routine became even more challenging when Simone became the first woman to deliver a triple-double in a major competition.

The move took a year to perfect and was a testament to how, in that time, she'd become an even more daring Simone Biles. It calls for two flips in layout position with three twists. It nearly defies physics and required Simone to reach at least ten feet off the mat at her highest point.

The video of the triple-double went viral, people all over the world trying to break it down in slow motion and figure out how this was even physically possible. Simone was one of the people watching the video. After completing her routine, she and Laurent took out her phone to see the replay.

"I didn't want to be the last person to see it," she said. "So, I went online to see what it looked like . . . I was very pleased."

It was quite a statement about the level she had reached, where she had come from, how abuse and challenges wouldn't hold her back, how she'd become a force of positivity, dedication, and superior skill. Maybe most importantly, it was a signal of where she was headed in 2020, where another Olympic stage awaited.

Of course, maybe Simone's greatest statement at the 2019 National Championships came when she warmed up in a custom leotard with a design only she could rock. There was the image of a goat—standing for the abbreviation G.O.A.T.

"Greatest Of All Time."

By that point, there was no one who could say otherwise.

# Instant
# Replay

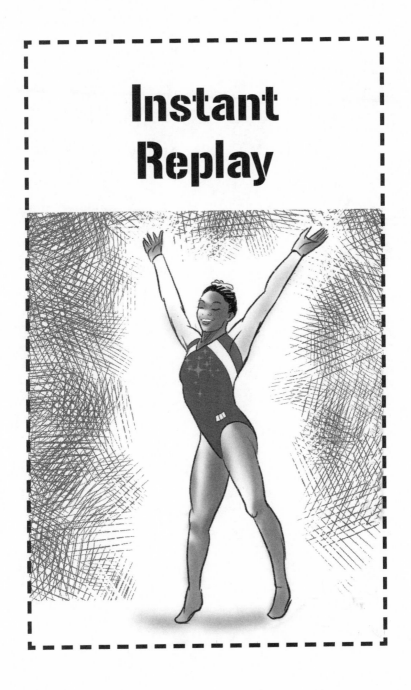

THE 2016 OLYMPICS WOMEN'S GYMNASTICS
ALL-AROUND FINAL

SIMONE'S FIRST TUMBLING PASS INCLUDES A DOUBLE LAYOUT WITH A HALF TWIST THAT HAS OFFICIALLY BECOME KNOWN AS "THE BILES."

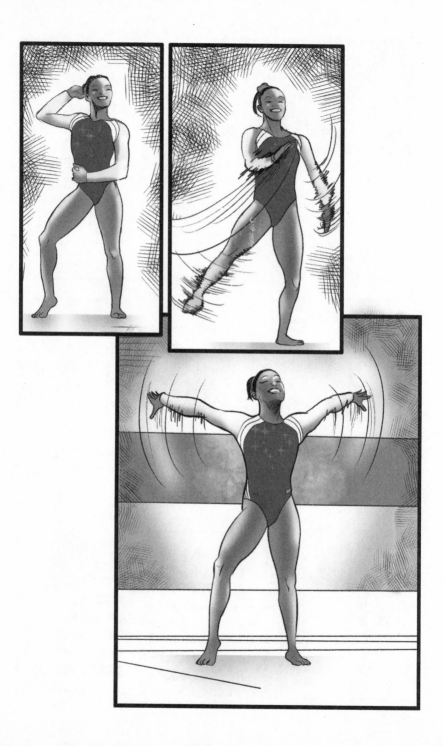

AFTER A MIDAIR SPLIT, SIMONE LEAPS WITH HER ARMS OUTSTRETCHED.

SIMONE HAS BEEN PREPARING FOR THIS MOMENT SINCE SHE WAS SIX YEARS OLD.

SHE FINISHES HER AMAZING ROUTINE WITH A BIT OF FLAIR.

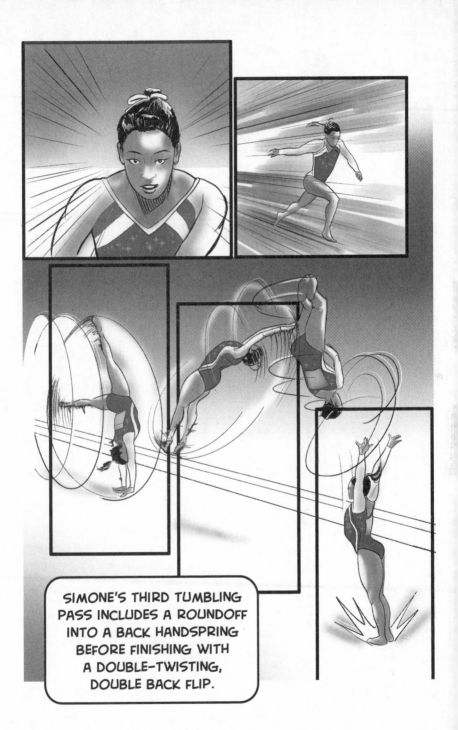

SIMONE'S THIRD TUMBLING PASS INCLUDES A ROUNDOFF INTO A BACK HANDSPRING BEFORE FINISHING WITH A DOUBLE-TWISTING, DOUBLE BACK FLIP.

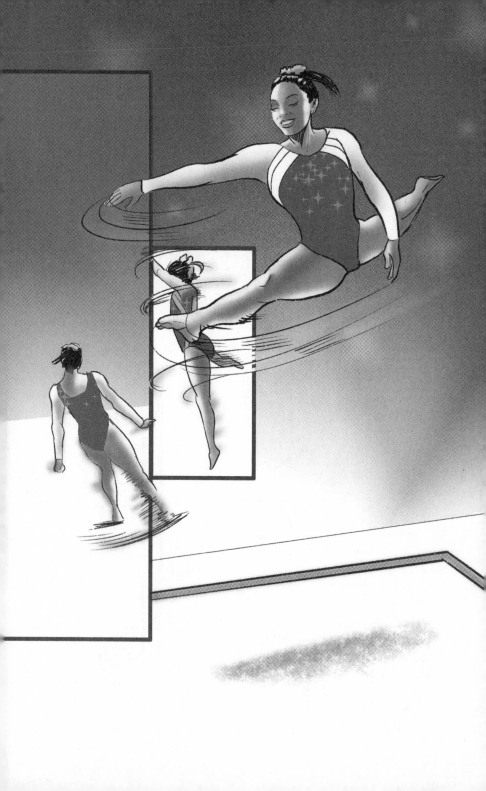